play guitar today!

T0071356

PLAYBACK+
Speed • Pitch • Balance • Loop

To access audio and video visit:
www.halleonard.com/mylibrary/proline

Enter Code
3946-7796-9871-7940

ISBN 978-1-5400-4573-7

HAL•LEONARD®

Visit Hal Leonard Online at
www.halleonard.com

Contact us:
Hal Leonard
7777 West Bluemound Road
Milwaukee, WI 53213
Email: info@halleonard.com

In Europe, contact:
Hal Leonard Europe Limited
42 Wigmore Street
Marylebone, London, W1U 2RN
Email: info@halleonardeurope.com

In Australia, contact:
Hal Leonard Australia Pty. Ltd.
4 Lentara Court
Cheltenham, Victoria, 3192 Australia
Email: info@halleonard.com.au

Introduction

Welcome to *Play Guitar Today!*—the series designed to prepare you for any style of guitar playing, from rock to blues to jazz to classical. Whatever your taste in music, *Play Guitar Today!* will give you the start you need.

About the Audio & Video

It's easy and fun to play guitar, and the accompanying audio will make your learning even more enjoyable, as we take you step by step through each lesson and play each song along with a full band. Much like with a real lesson, the best way to learn this material is to read and practice a while first on your own, then listen to the audio. With *Play Guitar Today!*, you can learn at your own pace. If there is ever something that you don't quite understand the first time through, go back to the audio and listen again. Every musical track has been given a track number, so if you want to practice a song again, you can find it right away.

Some lessons in the book include a video lesson, so you can see and hear the material being taught. Audio and videos are indicated with icons.

 Audio Icon   Video Icon

Contents

The Basics

Track 1

The Parts of the Guitar

The guitar has been a popular instrument for hundreds of years because it is both versatile and portable—not to mention it sounds great!

Although there are many different kinds of guitars, they all fall into one of two basic categories: **acoustic** or **electric**. These two types are shown to the right. Find the one that most resembles your own guitar, and get acquainted with its parts.

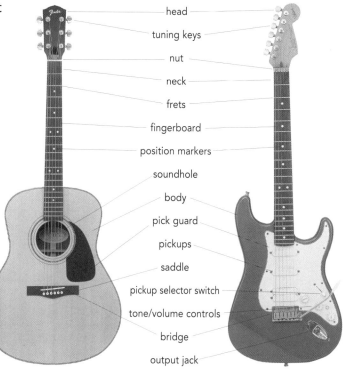

head
tuning keys
nut
neck
frets
fingerboard
position markers
soundhole
body
pick guard
pickups
saddle
pickup selector switch
tone/volume controls
bridge
output jack

acoustic　　　　　　　　　　　electric

How to Hold Your Guitar

Track 2

Sitting is probably the most comfortable position when first learning to play. Rest the guitar on your right thigh and hold it against the right side of your chest with your right arm. If you want to raise the neck to a more comfortable position, cross your legs—or find yourself a foot rest.

If your guitar has a strap, you may prefer to stand. The basic position of the guitar should remain the same. Your hands must always be free to move across the strings. Therefore, don't hold the guitar with your hands; support it with your body or with a strap.

Your Right and Left Hands

When you play, you'll be striking the strings with a pick held in your right hand. To hold the pick properly, grip it between the thumb and index finger, keeping the rest of your hand relaxed and your fingers curved. The fingers not holding the pick may rest on the guitar for extra support.

Your left hand belongs on the neck of the guitar. It, too, should be relaxed. To help you get a feel for the correct hand placement, follow these suggestions:

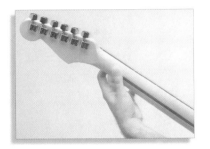

1. Place your thumb on the underside of the guitar neck.

2. Arch your fingers so that you will be able to reach all the strings more easily.

3. Avoid letting the palm of your hand touch the neck of the guitar.

Playing is Easy

You produce sounds on your guitar either by **strumming** several strings at once or by **picking** one string at a time. Take a minute to get a feel for this. With the pick in your right hand, use a downward motion and gently strum the strings. Practice this several times to get the feel of the pick and the strings. Then try picking the strings one at a time from bottom to top.

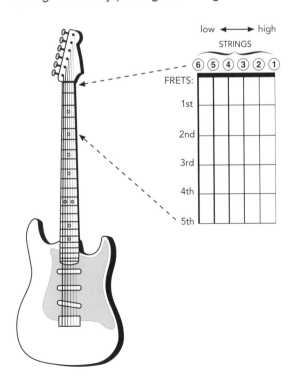

Notice that some strings sound higher and some sound lower? Each has a different **pitch**. Pitch is the highness or lowness of a sound. On the guitar, the strings are numbered 1 through 6, from the highest-sounding string (the thinnest) to the lowest-sounding one (the thickest).

As you can see, the frets of the guitar are also numbered, from low (near the nut) to high (near the bridge). Fretting higher up the neck produces sounds of a higher pitch, fretting lower on the neck produces sounds of a lower pitch.

The fingers of your left hand are also numbered, for convenience:

Track 3

Tuning Up

If you loosen a string by turning its tuning key, the pitch will become lower; if you tighten the string, the pitch will become higher. When two pitches sound exactly the same, they are said to be *in tune*. There are many ways to get your guitar in tune: you may use an electronic tuner, a piano, a pitch pipe, a tuning fork—you can even tune your guitar purely to itself. For now, however, listen to the audio to help you tune your instrument. The guitar's six open strings should be tuned to these pitches:

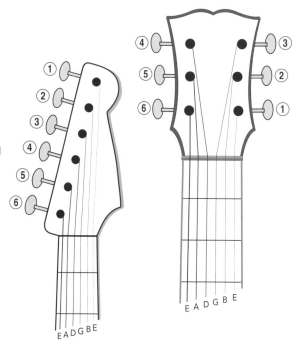

⑥ ⑤ ④ ③ ② ①
E–A–D–G–B–E
low ⟵⟶ high

Here are a few tips to help get you started:

- Whether tightening or loosening a string, turn the peg slowly so that you can concentrate on the changes in pitch. You may need to pick the string repeatedly to compare it.

- As you're tuning a string, you may notice that a series of pulsating **beat waves** becomes audible. These beat waves can actually help you tune: they'll slow down as you get closer to bringing two pitches together, and they'll stop completely once the two pitches are exactly the same.

- Instead of tuning a string down to pitch, tune it up. Tuning up allows you to stretch the string into place, which will help it stay in tune longer. So, if you begin with a string that is too high in pitch, tune it down first, and then bring it back up to pitch.

Another Way to Tune Your Guitar

1. Tune the 6th string E to a piano, a pitch pipe, an electronic tuner, or the track. If none of these is available, approximate E as best you can.
2. Press the 6th string at the 5th fret. This is A. Tune the open 5th string to this pitch.
3. Press the 5th string at the 5th fret. This is D. Tune the open 4th string to this pitch.
4. Press the 4th string at the 5th fret. This is G. Tune the open 3rd string to this pitch.
5. Press the 3rd string at the 4th fret. This is B. Tune the open 2nd string to this pitch.
6. Press the 2nd string at the 5th fret. This is E. Tune the open 1st string to this pitch.

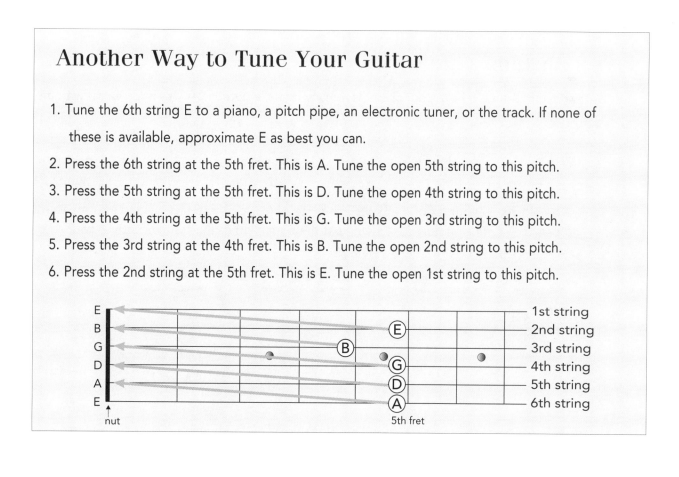

How to Read Music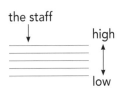

Musical sounds are indicated by symbols called *notes*. Notes come in all shapes and sizes, but every note has two important components: pitch and rhythm.

Pitch

Pitch (the highness or lowness of a note) is indicated by the placement of the note on a *staff*, a set of five lines and four spaces. Notes higher on the staff are higher in pitch; notes lower on the staff are lower in pitch.

To name the notes on the staff, we use the first seven letters of the alphabet: *A–B–C–D–E–F–G*. Adding a *treble clef* assigns a particular note name to each line and space on the staff, centered around the pitch G, the second line of the staff.

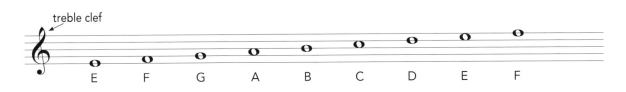

An easy way to remember the pitches on the lines is "**E**very **G**ood **B**oy **D**oes **F**ine." For the spaces, spell "FACE."

Rhythm

Rhythm refers to how long, or for how many beats, a note lasts. This is indicated with the following symbols:

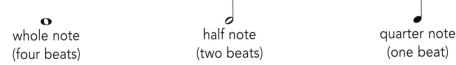

To help you keep track of the beats in a piece of music, the staff is divided into *measures* (or "bars"). A *time signature* (or "meter") at the beginning of the staff indicates how many beats you can expect to find in each measure.

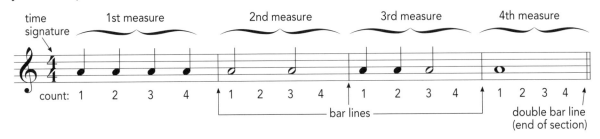

4/4 is perhaps the most common time signature. The top number ("4") tells you how many beats there are in each measure; the bottom number ("4") tells you what type of note value receives one beat. In 4/4 time, there are four beats in each measure, and each beat is worth one quarter note.

The First String: E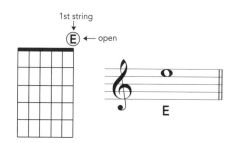

Track 4

The first three notes we'll learn on the guitar are all found on the high E string.

E

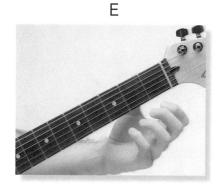

■ Your first note, E, is an "open-string" tone. There's nothing to fret—simply strike the open first string with your pick.

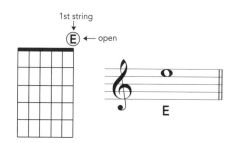

F

▶ Notice that your finger actually belongs directly behind each fret. If you place it on top of the fret, or too far back, you'll have difficulty getting a full, clear sound.

■ For the next note F, place your first finger on the first string directly behind the first fret, and strike the string with your pick.

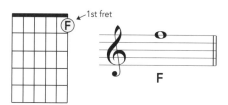

G

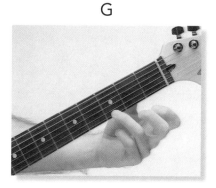

■ To play the note G, place your third finger on the first string directly behind the third fret, and strike the string with your pick.

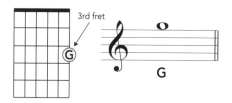

Learn to recognize these notes both on the fretboard and on the staff. Then, when you're comfortable playing the notes individually, try this short exercise. Speak the note names aloud as you play (e.g., "E, F, G, F...).

Track 5

E–F–G

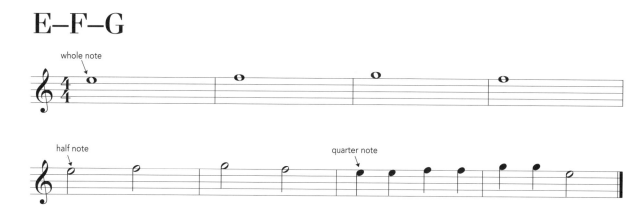

Of course, the best way to really learn these notes is to use them in some tunes. So let's do it. Start slowly with the following melodies, and concentrate on keeping your tempo nice and even. Practice these several times on your own before you try playing along with the audio.

Track 6

First Song

Keeping Time

Having trouble keeping a steady rhythm? Try tapping and counting along with each song. If the guitar is resting on your right leg, use your left foot to tap. Each time the foot comes down marks one beat. In 4/4 time, tap your foot four times in each measure, and count "1, 2, 3, 4." The first beat of each measure should be accented slightly—this is indicated below by the symbol ">."

count and tap: 1   2   3   4   1   2   3   4   1   2   3   4   1   2   3   4

Track 7

Second Song

► If you like, read through each song without your guitar at first: Tap the beat with your foot, count out loud, and clap through the rhythms.

Track 8

Third Song

8

Even though you don't actually use your left hand to fret the open string E, keep that hand on the guitar in "ready position," with your thumb on the back of the neck. This will allow you to fret the other notes that much more quickly.

Three-Note Rock

Track 9

Spiraling Downward

Track 10

► Try to keep your eyes on the page, instead of on your guitar.

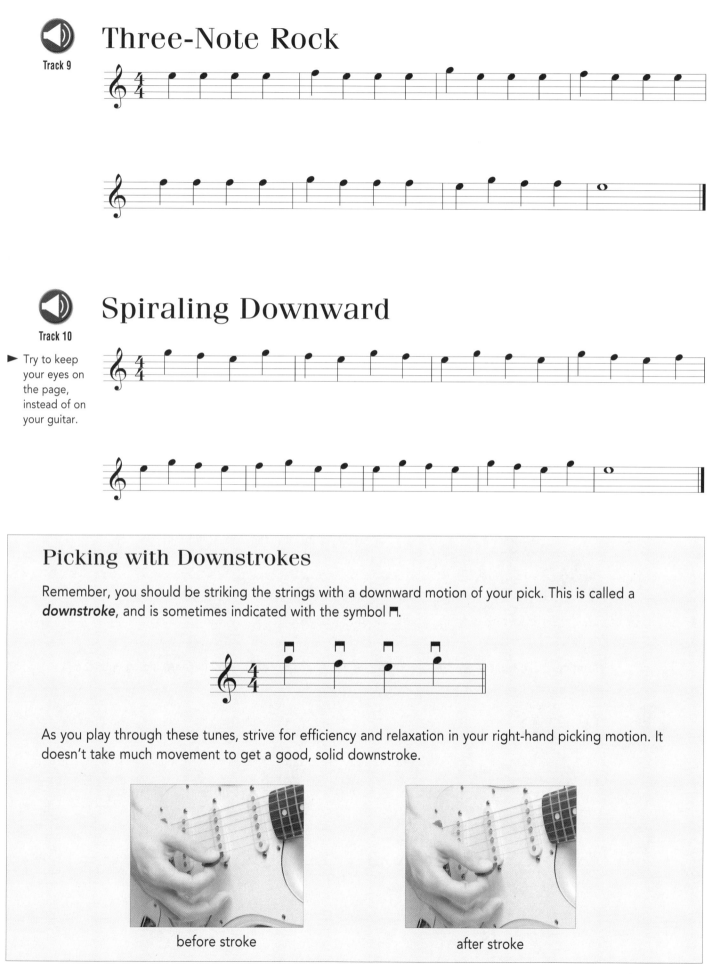

Picking with Downstrokes

Remember, you should be striking the strings with a downward motion of your pick. This is called a *downstroke*, and is sometimes indicated with the symbol ⊓.

As you play through these tunes, strive for efficiency and relaxation in your right-hand picking motion. It doesn't take much movement to get a good, solid downstroke.

before stroke

after stroke

The Second String: B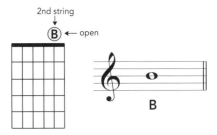

Track 11

Your next three notes are all played on the second string, B. You might want to check your tuning on that string before going any further.

► Notice that we're using the same fret positions as on the E string: open, 1st, and 3rd.

B

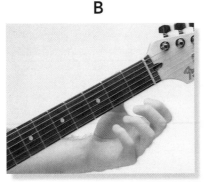

■ To play the note B, just strike the open second string.

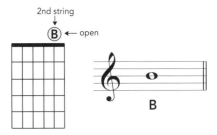

C

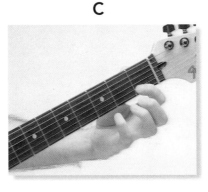

■ To play the note C, place your first finger on the second string directly behind the first fret.

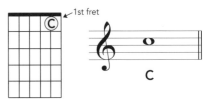

D

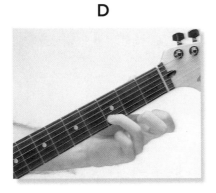

■ To play the note D, place your third finger on the second string directly behind the third fret.

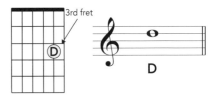

Practice these next exercises several times, slow and easy. Then play them along with the audio.

Track 12

B-C-D

TIP: Be sure to keep your left-hand fingers curved but relaxed, and use just your fingertips to fret the notes. Here's a test: you should be able to play any note on the B string, without muffling the open E above it. If you can't do this, you're probably laying your fingers too flat across the fretboard.

Three to Get Ready

Track 13

Now here are some tunes to practice all six notes you've learned so far. Don't be afraid to review E, F, and G again before tackling these!

Two-String Rock

Track 14

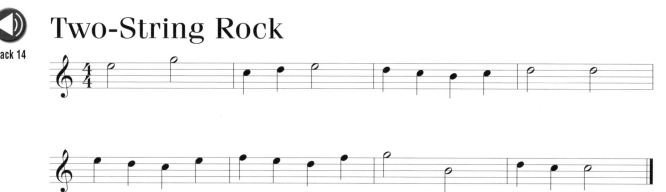

Fingering Tip

When moving from a lower note to a higher note on the same string, try leaving the lower note depressed. For example, on the first string, leave your first finger on F while you put your third finger on G. Now, to go back to F, you simply lift your third finger. This way, you don't have to find the first fret all over again—you're already there!

Ode to Joy

Track 15

Jingle Bells

Black Dog Blues

► This song moves from string to string a lot. Be careful and start slowly.

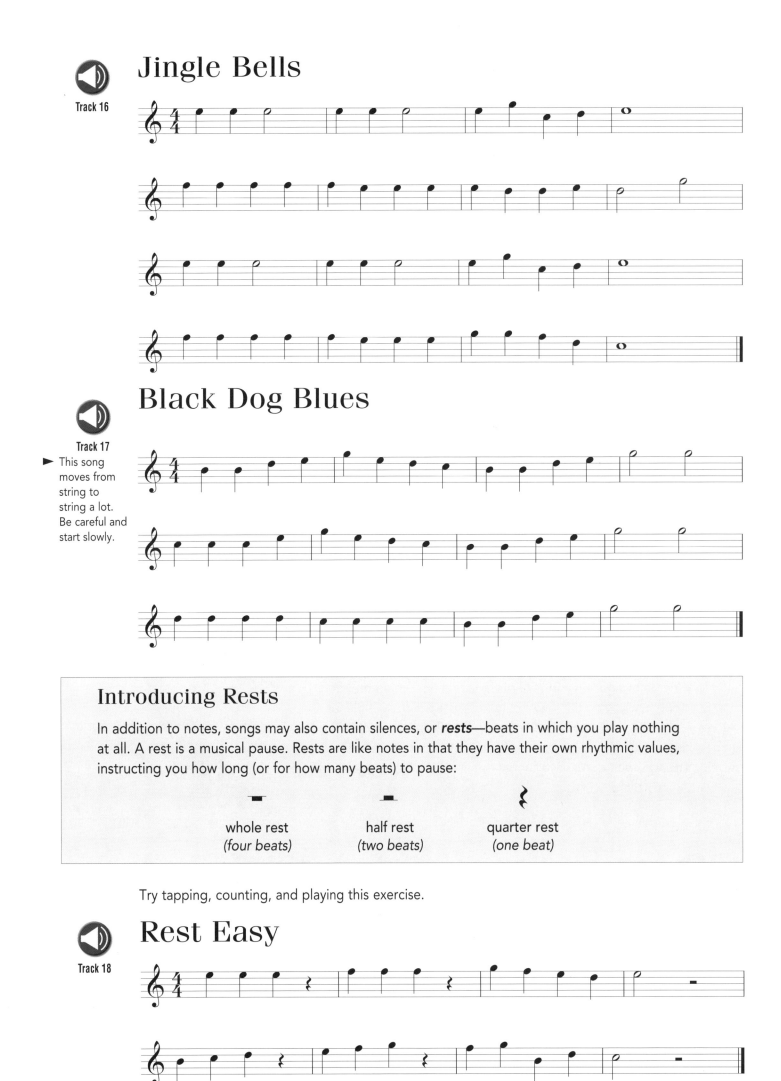

Introducing Rests

In addition to notes, songs may also contain silences, or **rests**—beats in which you play nothing at all. A rest is a musical pause. Rests are like notes in that they have their own rhythmic values, instructing you how long (or for how many beats) to pause:

whole rest
(four beats)

half rest
(two beats)

quarter rest
(one beat)

Try tapping, counting, and playing this exercise.

Rest Easy

Here's something else to consider: When you encounter a rest, you may need to stop any previous notes from sounding. To do this, try the following:

- For an open-string note, like E, touch the string lightly with your left-hand finger(s).
- For a fretted note, like F, decrease the pressure of your left-hand finger on the string.

Rock 'n' Rest

Track 19

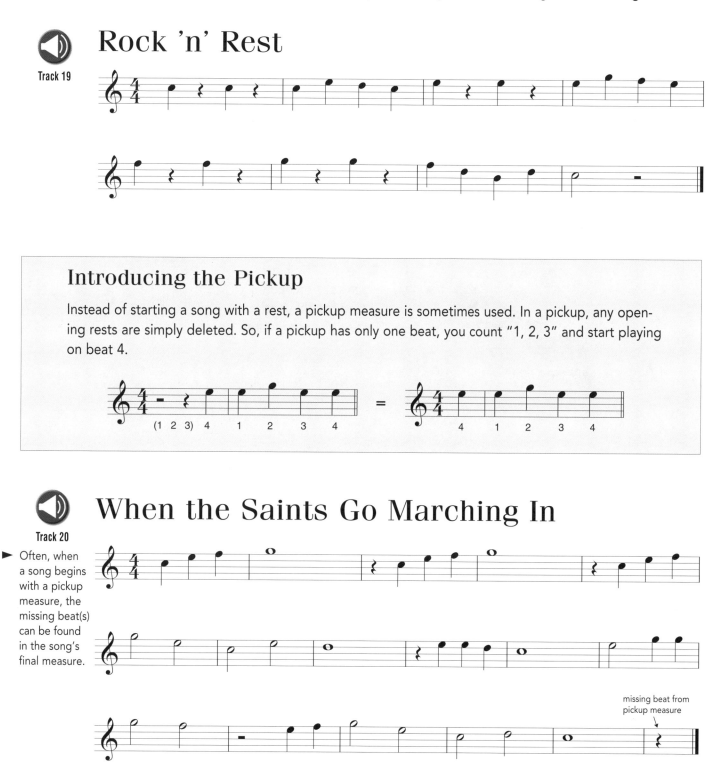

Introducing the Pickup

Instead of starting a song with a rest, a pickup measure is sometimes used. In a pickup, any opening rests are simply deleted. So, if a pickup has only one beat, you count "1, 2, 3" and start playing on beat 4.

When the Saints Go Marching In

Track 20

► Often, when a song begins with a pickup measure, the missing beat(s) can be found in the song's final measure.

missing beat from pickup measure

By the way, it's much better to practice just a little every day than it is to cram everything into one long session—your fingers and your mind need time to develop.

The Third String: G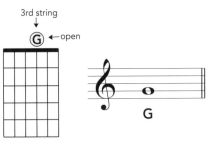

Track 21

For this string, we'll learn just two notes, including one that's on the second fret. Don't forget to check your tuning.

G

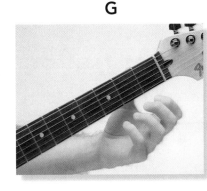

► Notice that we're learning another G note—since the musical alphabet contains only the letters A through G, this type of repetition will eventually occur with all the note names.

■ To play the note G, strike the open third string.

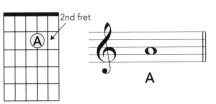

A

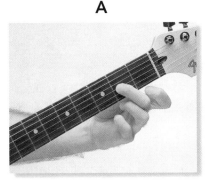

■ To play the note A, place your second finger on the third string, behind the second fret.

Let's practice our two new notes, G and A.

Track 22

Two-Note Jam

Three-String Review

Here's all the notes we've learned so far, from G to G. That's eight notes in all!

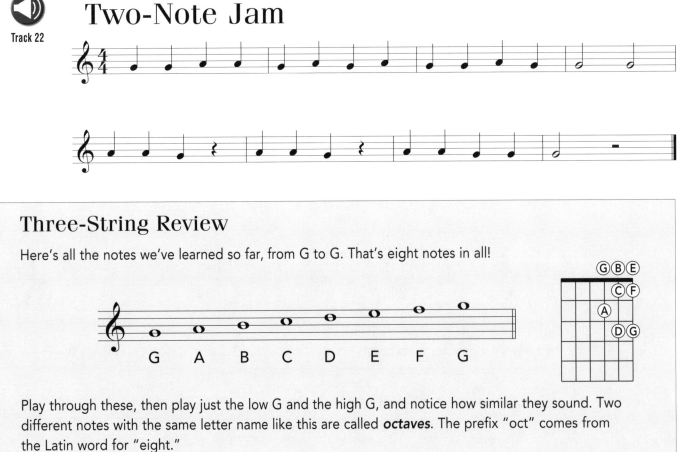

G A B C D E F G

Play through these, then play just the low G and the high G, and notice how similar they sound. Two different notes with the same letter name like this are called *octaves*. The prefix "oct" comes from the Latin word for "eight."

Remember to practice these next songs slowly at first. Ideally, you should be able to read and play the notes in time, without having to slow down or stop in the middle of a song. Speed up the tempo as you become more confident with the notes, and then play along with the band.

Track 23

Brother John

Track 24

Red River Rock

► Notice the pickup measure on this song. You actually begin playing on beat 3.

Track 25

Aura Lee

► Try this: put your guitar down and just recite the note names of the song ("G, C, B, C, D, A, D...").

Track 26

Michael, Row Your Boat Ashore

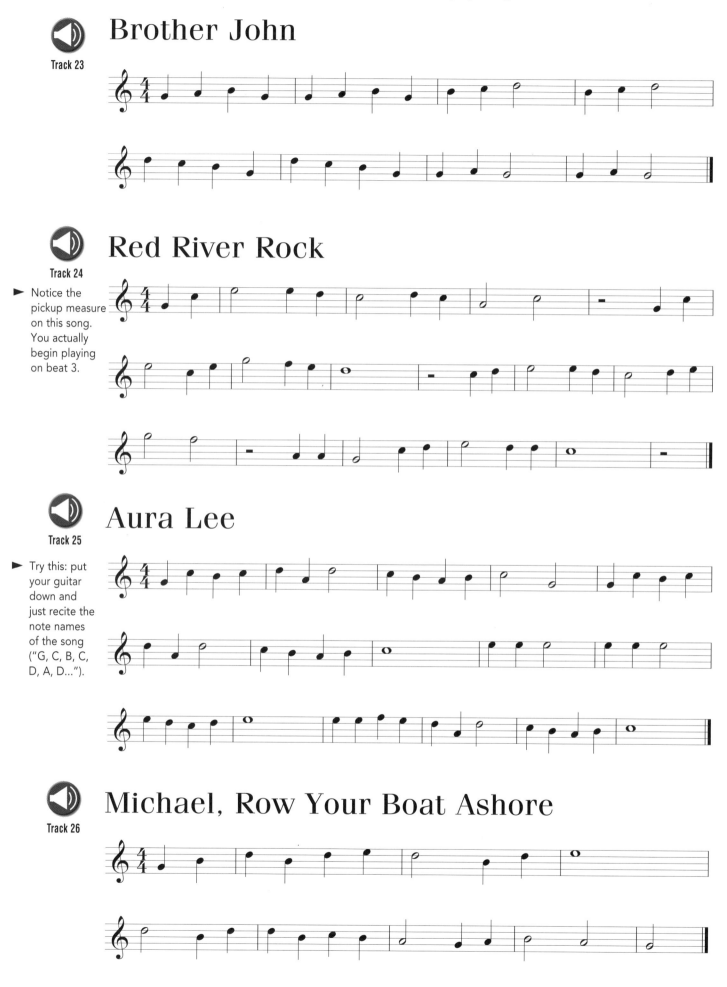

15

Here Comes the Guitarist

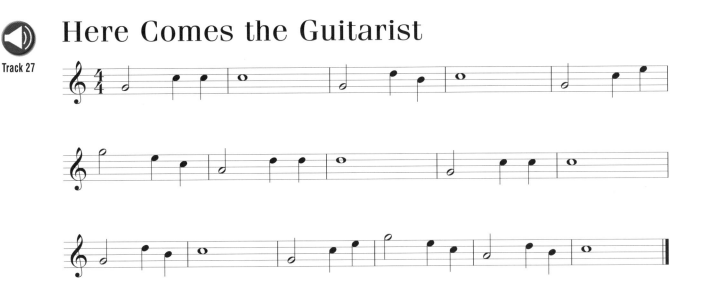

If your fingertips hurt, take a break. The more you practice, the faster they'll toughen up, but it takes time.

Two New Notes: F♯ and C♯

Notice that we skipped the second fret on both the first and second strings. Let's go back and grab those notes.

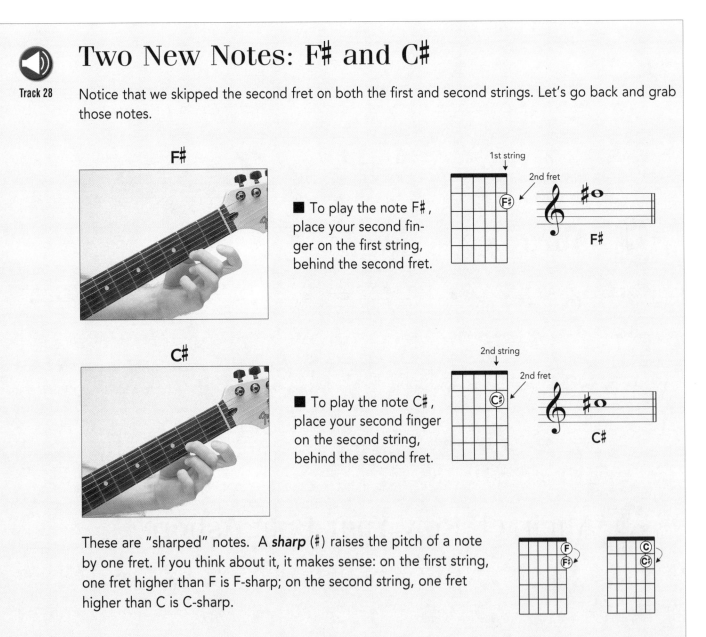

F♯

■ To play the note F♯, place your second finger on the first string, behind the second fret.

1st string
2nd fret
F♯

C♯

■ To play the note C♯, place your second finger on the second string, behind the second fret.

2nd string
2nd fret
C♯

These are "sharped" notes. A *sharp* (♯) raises the pitch of a note by one fret. If you think about it, it makes sense: on the first string, one fret higher than F is F-sharp; on the second string, one fret higher than C is C-sharp.

16

Sharps, Flats, and Naturals

Sharps are part of a group of musical symbols called **accidentals**, which raise or lower the pitch of a note:

A **sharp** (♯) raises the pitch of a note by one fret.

A **flat** (♭) lowers the pitch of a note by one fret.

A **natural** (♮) cancels a previous sharp or flat, returning a note to its original pitch.

In musical terms, the distance of one fret is called a **half step**. When a song requires a note to be a half step higher or lower, you'll see a sharp (♯), flat (♭), or natural (♮) sign in front of it. This tells you to raise or lower the note for that measure only. We'll see more of these "accidentals" as we continue learning more notes on the guitar.

Track 29

► Try this short exercise with your new notes.

Sharpen Up

Track 30

Rockin' Sharps

Track 31

► Once again, try to keep your eyes on the music, not your fingers.

Secret Agent Sharp

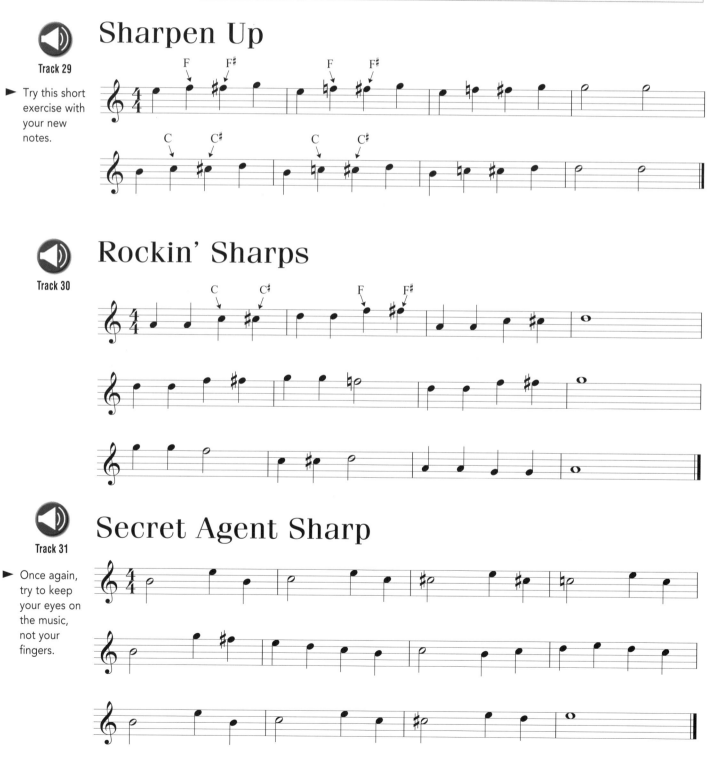

The Fourth String: D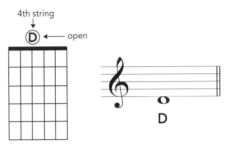

The fourth string is like the third string in that we'll skip over the first fret—but this time we'll get three notes.

Track 32

D

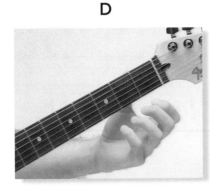

■ To play the note D, strike the open fourth string.

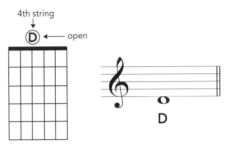

E

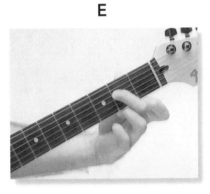

■ To play the note E, place your second finger on the fourth string, behind the second fret.

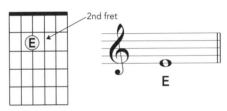

F

► Sound familiar? The new D, E, and F, sound one octave lower than the old D, E, and F.

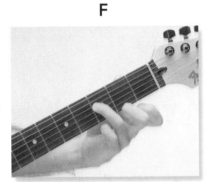

■ To play the note F, place your third finger on the fourth string, behind the third fret.

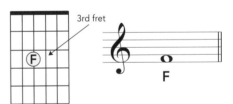

Track 33

D-E-F

D-String Riff

Track 34

► The word riff is slang for a repeated instrumental figure, or musical idea.

Now, try your new notes in some more songs. Practice them slowly at first.

Easy Does It

Track 35

Crosswalk Blues

Track 36

► If you like, let the D string ring out on this song.

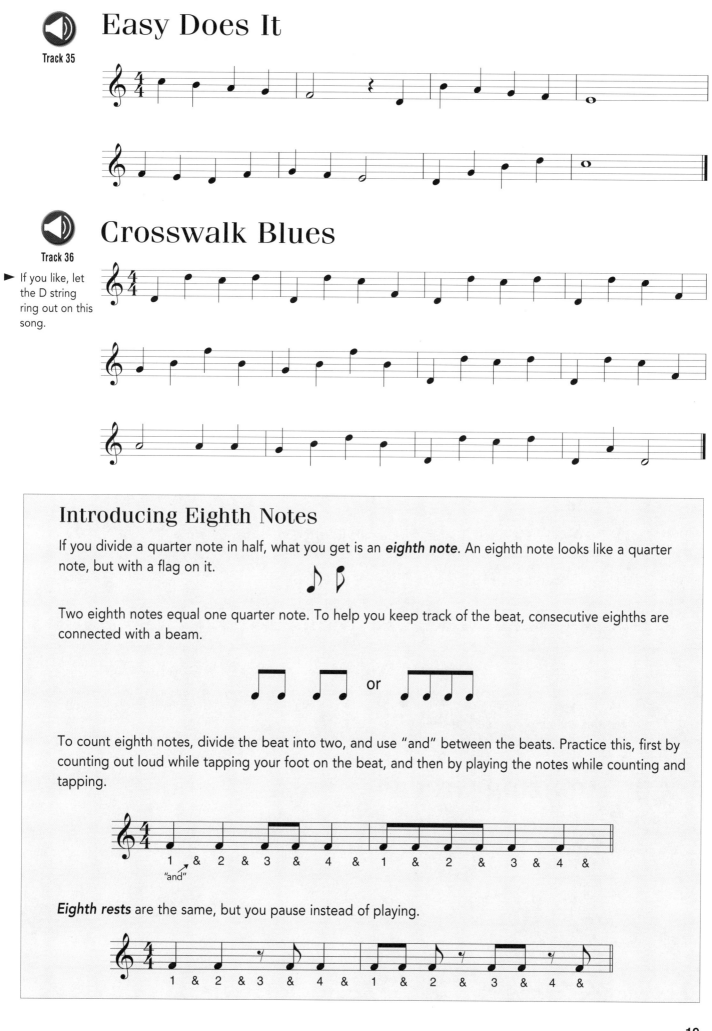

Introducing Eighth Notes

If you divide a quarter note in half, what you get is an *eighth note*. An eighth note looks like a quarter note, but with a flag on it.

Two eighth notes equal one quarter note. To help you keep track of the beat, consecutive eighths are connected with a beam.

or

To count eighth notes, divide the beat into two, and use "and" between the beats. Practice this, first by counting out loud while tapping your foot on the beat, and then by playing the notes while counting and tapping.

1 &   2 &   3 &   4 &   1 &   2 &   3 &   4 &

"and"

Eighth rests are the same, but you pause instead of playing.

1 & 2 & 3 & 4 &   1 & 2 & 3 & 4 &

Now try some songs that use eighth notes. Keep that foot tapping!

Alouette

Track 37

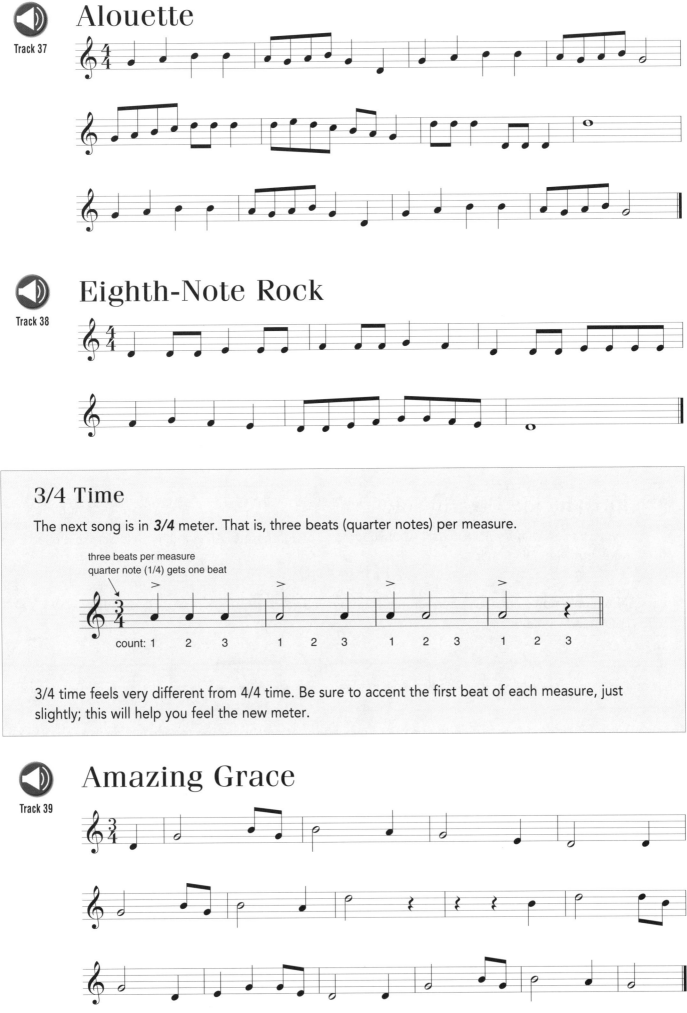

Eighth-Note Rock

Track 38

3/4 Time

The next song is in **3/4** meter. That is, three beats (quarter notes) per measure.

three beats per measure
quarter note (1/4) gets one beat

count: 1   2   3   1   2   3   1   2   3   1   2   3

3/4 time feels very different from 4/4 time. Be sure to accent the first beat of each measure, just slightly; this will help you feel the new meter.

Amazing Grace

Track 39

Two More Notes: F♯ and B♭

From the strings that we already know, let's add two more new notes: F♯ and B♭.

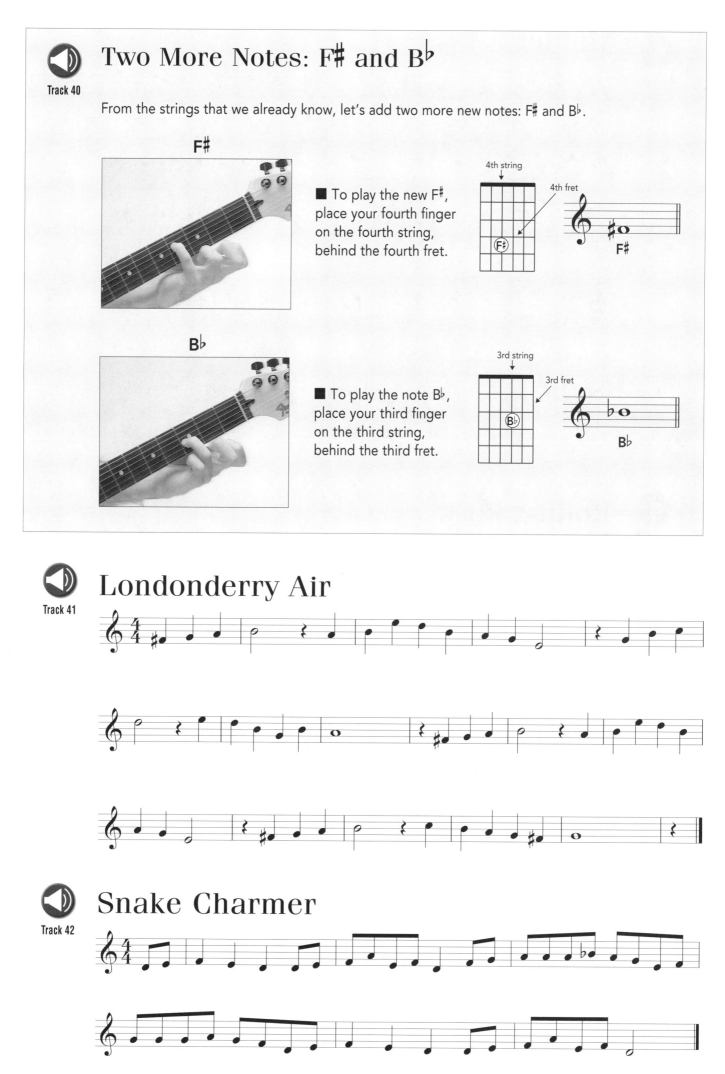

F♯

■ To play the new F♯, place your fourth finger on the fourth string, behind the fourth fret.

4th string

4th fret

F♯

B♭

■ To play the note B♭, place your third finger on the third string, behind the third fret.

3rd string

3rd fret

B♭

Londonderry Air

Snake Charmer

Minuet

Track 43

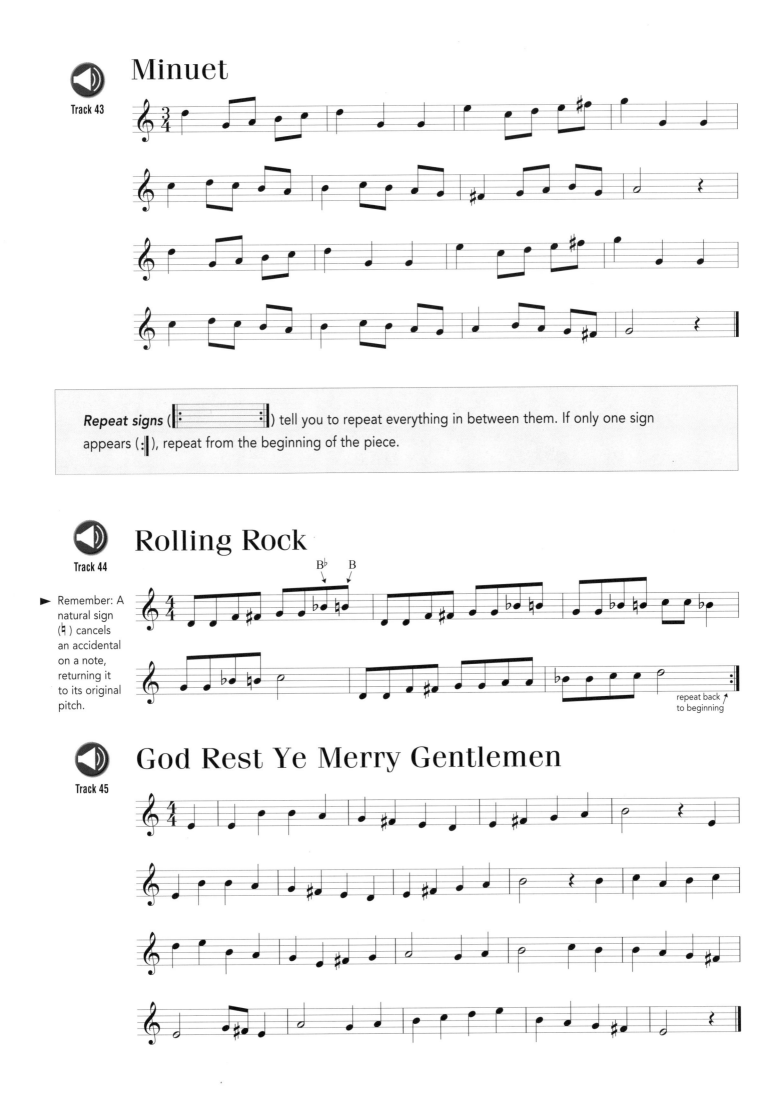

Repeat signs ( ) tell you to repeat everything in between them. If only one sign appears ( ), repeat from the beginning of the piece.

Rolling Rock

Track 44

► Remember: A natural sign (♮) cancels an accidental on a note, returning it to its original pitch.

repeat back to beginning

God Rest Ye Merry Gentlemen

Track 45

Bourrée

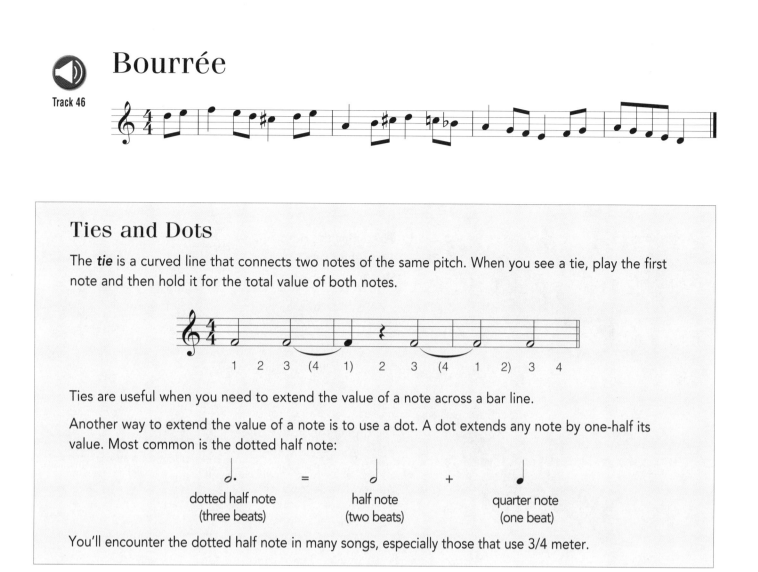

Ties and Dots

The *tie* is a curved line that connects two notes of the same pitch. When you see a tie, play the first note and then hold it for the total value of both notes.

1   2   3   (4   1)   2   3   (4   1   2)   3   4

Ties are useful when you need to extend the value of a note across a bar line.

Another way to extend the value of a note is to use a dot. A dot extends any note by one-half its value. Most common is the dotted half note:

dotted half note   =   half note   +   quarter note
(three beats)   (two beats)   (one beat)

You'll encounter the dotted half note in many songs, especially those that use 3/4 meter.

It Came Upon a Midnight Clear

The Fifth String: A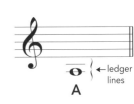

Track 48

Are you still in tune? Then it's time for another string. Your new notes, A, B, and C, are all played on the fifth string. Notice that these notes all make use of *ledger lines*, which extend the staff downward, allowing us to notate these lower pitches.

A

► Fingering-wise, the fifth string is just like the fourth: It uses open, 2nd, and 3rd fret positions.

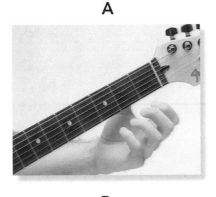

■ To play the note A, strike the open fifth string.

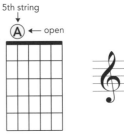

B

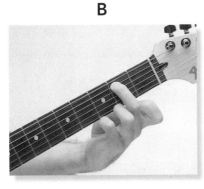

■ To play the note B, place your second finger on the fifth string, behind the second fret.

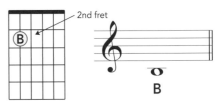

C

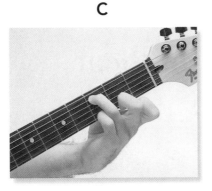

■ To play the note C, place your third finger on the fifth string, behind the third fret.

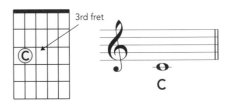

Practice your new A, B, and C. Take it slow.

Track 49

A-B-C

Cruisin'

Track 50

Surfin'

Track 51

Fallin' Down

Track 52

Greensleeves

Track 53

Nine Hundred Miles

Track 54

► This next song is in 2/4 time. That is, two beats (quarter notes) per measure.

Introducing Alternate Picking

Alternate picking (a.k.a "the down/up stroke") is a good way of adding speed and facility to your guitar playing. It's actually a combination of two separate movements:

Downstroke Plucking or strumming the strings *downward*. This is how we've been playing all our tunes up to now. You should continue to use a downstroke for all notes that fall on a strong beat: "1," "2," "3," or "4." Remember the downstroke symbol is "⊓."

Upstroke Plucking or strumming the strings *upward*. An upstroke is generally used for an eighth note that falls on the second half of the beat—on the "and." The symbol for upstroke is "V."

Try the following short exercises on the open high E string, using alternate picking.

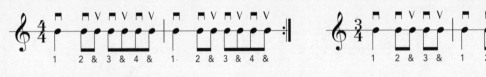

Boogie Blues

Track 55

► Now try this tune. First, play it with all downstrokes, then try the alternate picking method indicated.

26

The Sixth String: E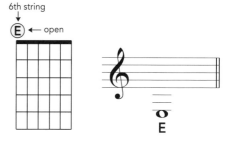

Track 56

The notes E, F, and G are played on the sixth string of the guitar. As you practice these new notes, memorize their positions on the ledger lines.

E

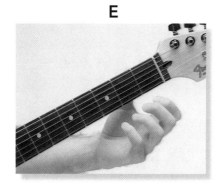

■ To play the note E, strike the open sixth string.

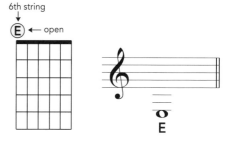

F

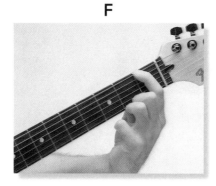

■ To play the note F, place your first finger on the sixth string, behind the first fret.

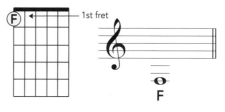

G

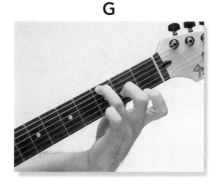

■ To play the note G, place your third finger on the sixth string, behind the third fret.

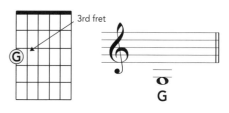

Same Notes, Different String

Notice anything familiar here? These are the exact same notes and fingerings you learned for the first string, just two octaves lower:

The trick here will be reading and memorizing these notes on the staff. All those ledger lines can be tough. By the way, there's another set of E, F, and G notes in between the first and sixth strings. Can you find it?

Take it nice and slow at first. Don't forget to let your eyes read ahead of the notes you're actually playing; this can especially help on those low strings.

Sixth-String Strut

Track 57

▶ Try alternate picking on successive eighth notes. Stick with downstrokes for any note that occurs on the beat.

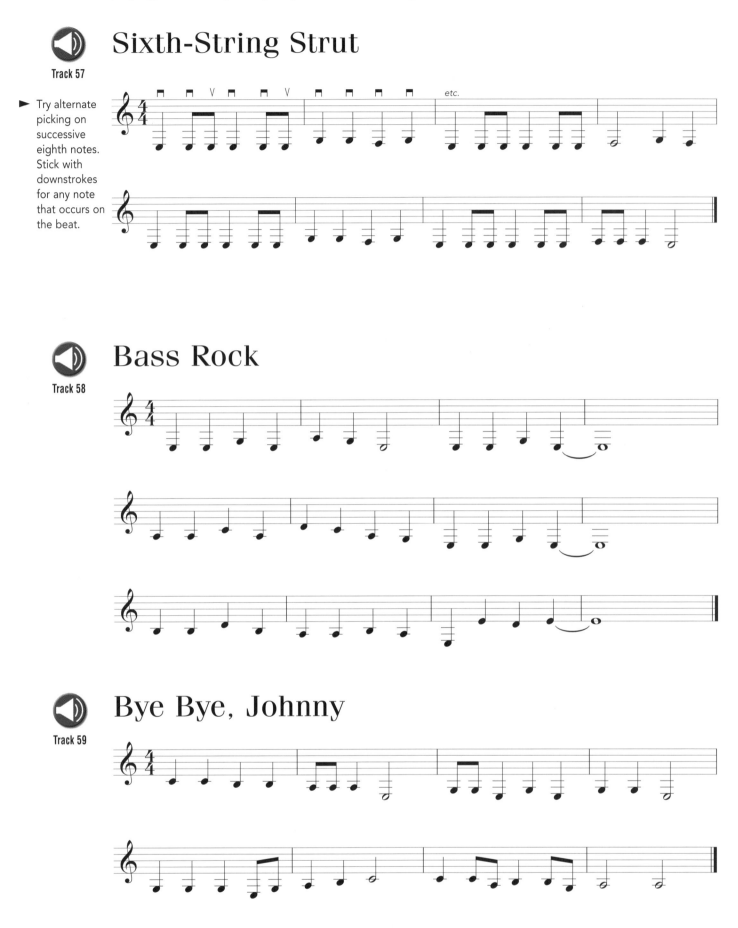

Bass Rock

Track 58

Bye Bye, Johnny

Track 59

The Dotted Quarter Note

As we know, a dot lengthens a note by one half its time value. When a quarter note is followed by a dot, its time value is increased from 1 beat to 1 1/2 beats.

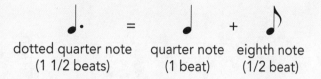

dotted quarter note   quarter note   eighth note
(1 1/2 beats)   (1 beat)   (1/2 beat)

A dotted quarter note is usually followed by an eighth note. This pattern has a total time value of two beats.

To get more comfortable with counting dotted quarter notes, try the following rhythm exercise:

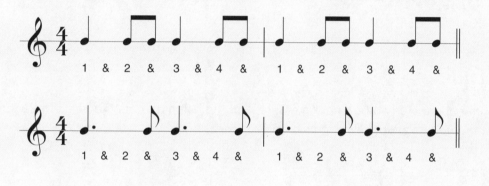

Rockin' Riff

Track 60

Hark! The Herald Angels Sing

Track 61

2/2 Time

In **2/2 time**, there are two beats per measure, and the half note gets the beat. This actually feels a lot like 4/4, but you only tap your foot twice in each measure.

1 & 2 &   1 & 2 &   1 e & a 2 e & a   1 & 2 &

Hail to the Guitarist

Track 62

More Notes: B♭ and E♭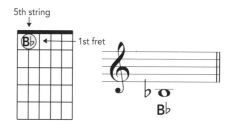

Track 63

We may have learned all six strings, but let's double back and pick up just a few more notes before we move on.

B♭

■ To play the note B♭, place your first finger on the fifth string, behind the first fret.

E♭

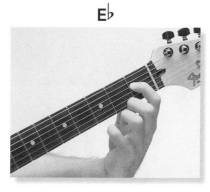

■ To play the note E♭, place your first finger on the fourth string, behind the first fret.

Track 64

Minor Jam

Track 65

Theme of Mystery

Silent Night

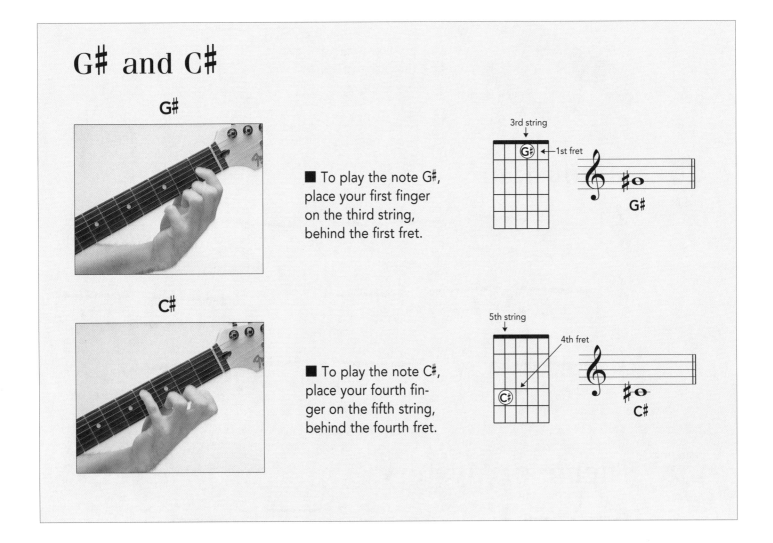

G♯ and C♯

G♯

■ To play the note G♯, place your first finger on the third string, behind the first fret.

3rd string

G♯ ← 1st fret

G♯

C♯

■ To play the note C♯, place your fourth finger on the fifth string, behind the fourth fret.

5th string

C♯ ← 4th fret

C♯

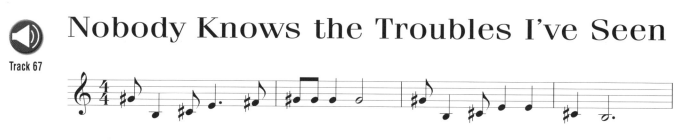

Nobody Knows the Troubles I've Seen

Track 67

John Brown's Body

Track 68

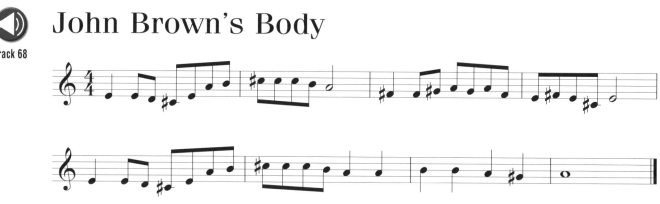

F♯ and G♯

These last two notes are both on the sixth string.

F♯

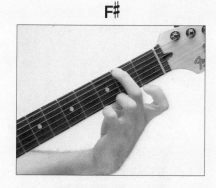

■ To play the note F♯, place your second finger on the sixth string, behind the second fret.

G♯

■ To play the note G♯, place your fourth finger on the sixth string, behind the fourth fret.

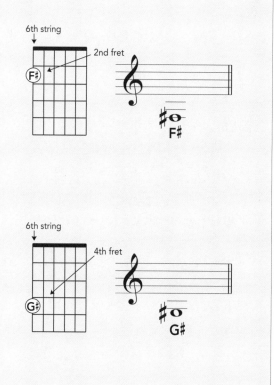

Blues in E

Track 69

Low Groove

Track 70

► Watch the notes on this one. Try to read *ahead* of the music.

Six-String Review

We've come a long way. In fact, we've learned just about *every note* in the guitar's open position. See if you can figure out the names of the two notes that we *haven't* covered.

Answer: E♭, G♯

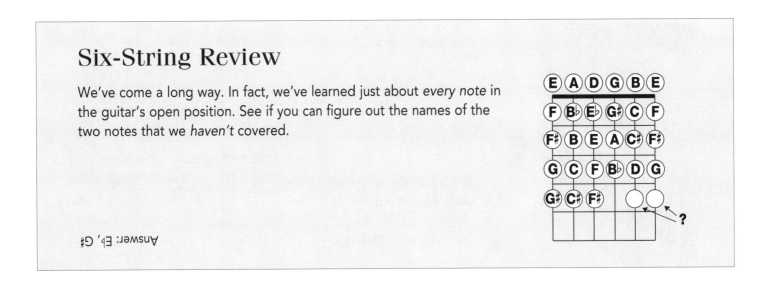

Major Chords

Track 71

Now that you've got a handle on all six strings, it's time to start learning about chords. *"What's a chord?"* you ask. A **chord** is three or more notes played simultaneously. We'll start off with three of the most common **major** chords. (More about what "major" means later...)

To play a chord, first get your left-hand fingers into position—the dots on each grid below tell you where to fret the strings, and the numbers tell you what fingers to use. Then, with your right hand, strum downward across the strings—but only those strings that are part of the chord. Xs above a grid tell you to avoid strumming a string. Os indicate an open string.

C

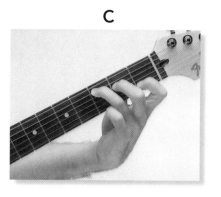

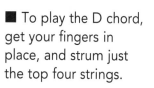 To play the C chord, get your fingers in place, then strum downward, starting on the fifth string.

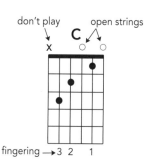

G

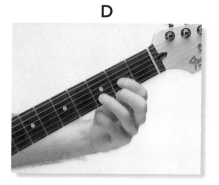

 To play the G chord, get your fingers in place, then strum across all six strings.

D

To play the D chord, get your fingers in place, and strum just the top four strings.

Troubleshooting Chords

If a chord sounds bad, try playing through it again, but slowly, one string at a time. If you find a "problem string," readjust your finger or your hand position, and try again.

- **Are your fingers curved?** If you let them fall flat, they'll block other strings from sounding.
- **Is your thumb on the back of the guitar neck?** This will help you apply pressure to all the strings.
- **Are your fingers directly behind the frets?** This will give you a good, clear tone.

Introducing Tablature or "TAB"

We'll be learning a new type of musical notation to go with chords called *tablature*, or *"TAB"* for short. It consists of six lines, one for each string of your guitar. The numbers written on the lines indicate which fret to play in order to sound the correct notes.

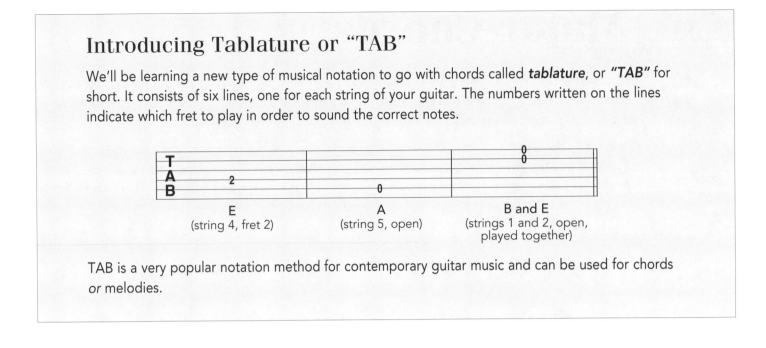

E	A	B and E
(string 4, fret 2)	(string 5, open)	(strings 1 and 2, open, played together)

TAB is a very popular notation method for contemporary guitar music and can be used for chords *or* melodies.

Tab This!

Track 72

Now try reading chords in notation and TAB.

Let's Strum

Track 73

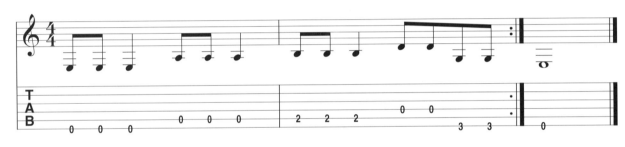

Let's Strum, Pt. 2

Track 74

The next step is to try mixing the chords up. Chords arranged in sequence like this are called **pro-gressions**. The number of possibilities are many. This chord progression moves from G to D to C to D and winds up back at G.

Track 75

Unplugged

► Don't be afraid to review these chords individually before playing this one!

Here are a few very common progressions based on the same three chords: G, C, and D. You may recognize the first one, as it's similar to many rock songs, including "Louie, Louie" and "Wild Thing."

Track 76

Wild Rock

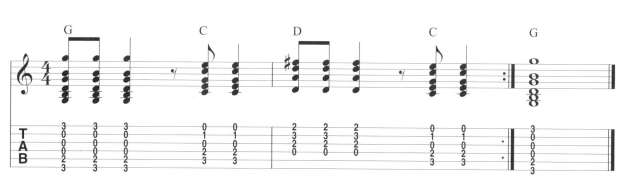

Track 77

Chord Moves

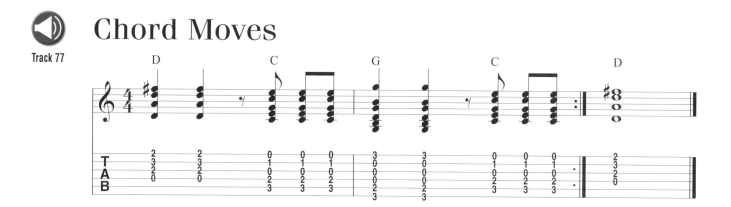

Chords can also be used to accompany a melody. Play the following songs by reading from the chord line. Strum once for each beat (that would be three strums per measure for the first two songs), and sing along with the melody.

Good Morning to All

Track 78

This next song is in 4/4 time, so strum four times per measure—or vary your strum pattern.

Buffalo Gals

Track 80

Minor Chords

Track 81

Since we just learned three major chords, let's even things out by learning three *minor* chords.

Em

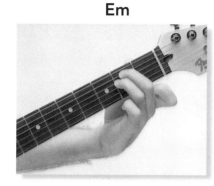

■ To play the Em chord, strum across all six strings.

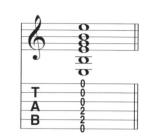

Am

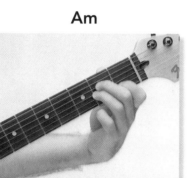

■ To play the Am, begin your strum with the fifth string.

Dm

■ To play the Dm chord, strum just the top four strings.

Major vs. Minor

The difference between major and minor chords is in how they sound. Take a minute to compare two major and minor chords—like D and Dm. Notice how each one makes you feel? It's difficult to put into words, but generally we say that major chords have a strong, upbeat, or happy quality, while minor chords have a darker, sadder quality.

D

Dm

In terms of reading them, just remember that major chords use just the letter name (e.g., D), but minor chords use letter name plus the suffix "m" (e.g., Dm).

Once again, when you feel comfortable with each chord individually, start experimenting with progressions.

Track 82

Let's Strum Again

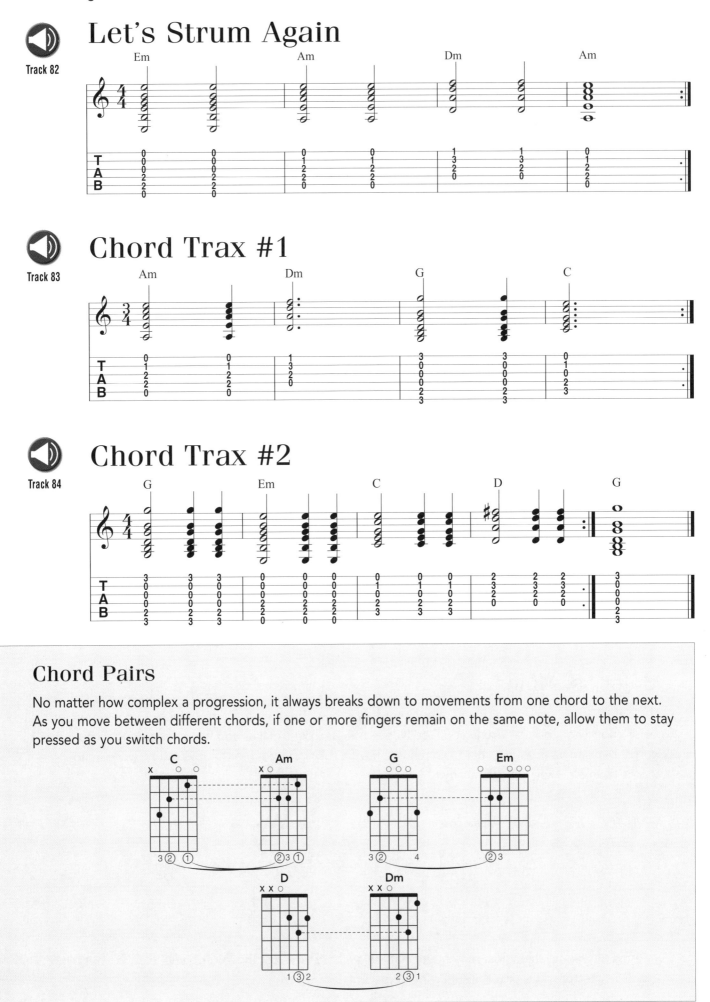

Track 83

Chord Trax #1

Chord Trax #2

Track 84

Chord Pairs

No matter how complex a progression, it always breaks down to movements from one chord to the next. As you move between different chords, if one or more fingers remain on the same note, allow them to stay pressed as you switch chords.

For the next example, try using an upstroke (v) for the last eighth note in each measure.

Chord Trax #3

Track 85

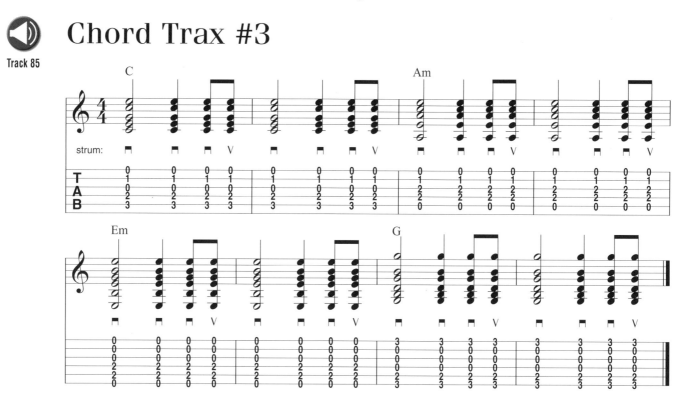

Strumming Partial Chords

When alternate strumming, don't worry about hitting every single note on the upstroke. Instead, just play two, three, or four notes of the chord—in other words, play whatever feels natural.

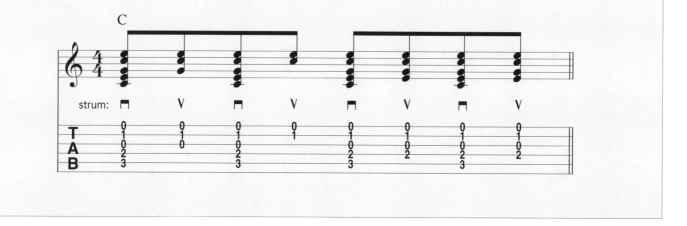

Chord Trax #4

Track 86

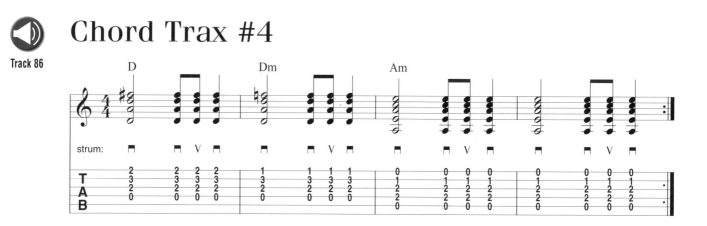

Chord Trax #5

Track 87

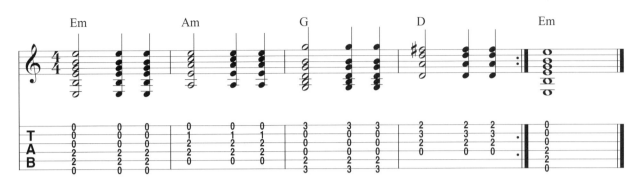

Once again, let's practice our new chords with some well-known melodies. Sing, and use the chord line to strum along.

Track 88

When Johnny Comes Marching Home

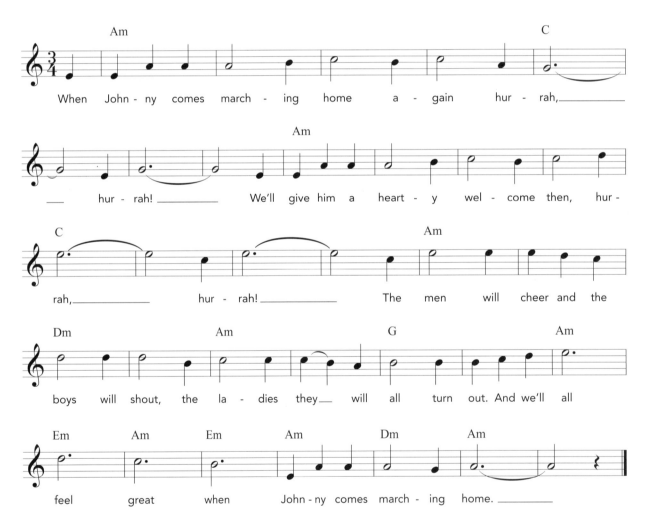

Scarborough Fair

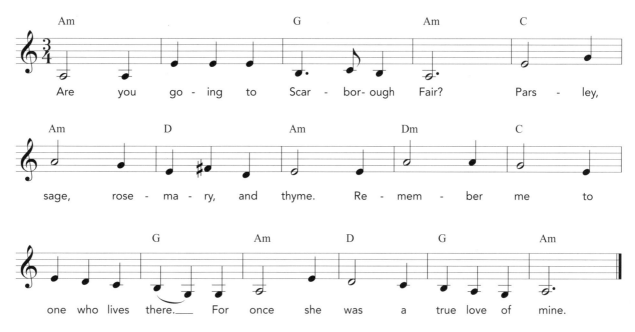

Slash Notation

Another way that you might see chord progressions written out is in **slash notation**. Slashes indicate how many beats each chord should be played; it's up to you to supply the strumming pattern. In the following progressions, first try strumming once for every slash (" **/** ") symbol. Then, follow the chord line and try variations of downstrokes and upstrokes.

Makin' Trax

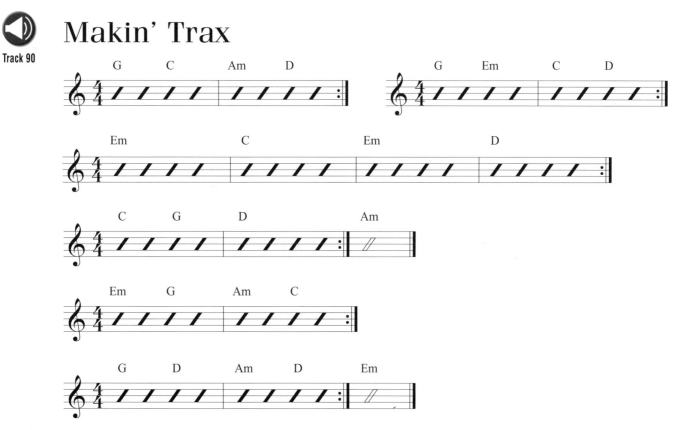

Practice chords daily (at least 15 minutes). Eventually, they'll become second nature. You'll instantly react when you see a chord symbol rather than trying to think of each fingering and note placement.

One More Note: A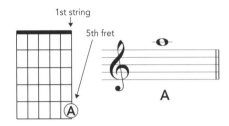

Track 91

Let's go back to that first string and grab one more note, the high A. This one will be played with the pinky.

A

■ To play the high A, place your fourth finger on the first string, behind the fifth fret.

You'll probably want to move your hand up the fretboard, just a bit, to reach that fifth fret. Otherwise, you can opt to keep your hand in place, and stretch to reach the note. It's your choice.

Track 92

Hittin' the High A

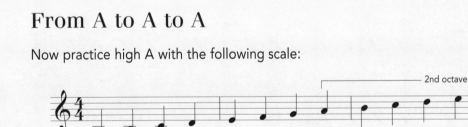

From A to A to A

Now practice high A with the following scale:

A *scale* is an arrangement of notes in a specific, sequential pattern. Most scales use eight notes, with the top and the bottom notes being an octave apart. The one above spans two octaves.

And now a few more familiar tunes.

Home Sweet Home

Track 93

Auld Lang Syne

Track 94

House of the Rising Sun

Track 95

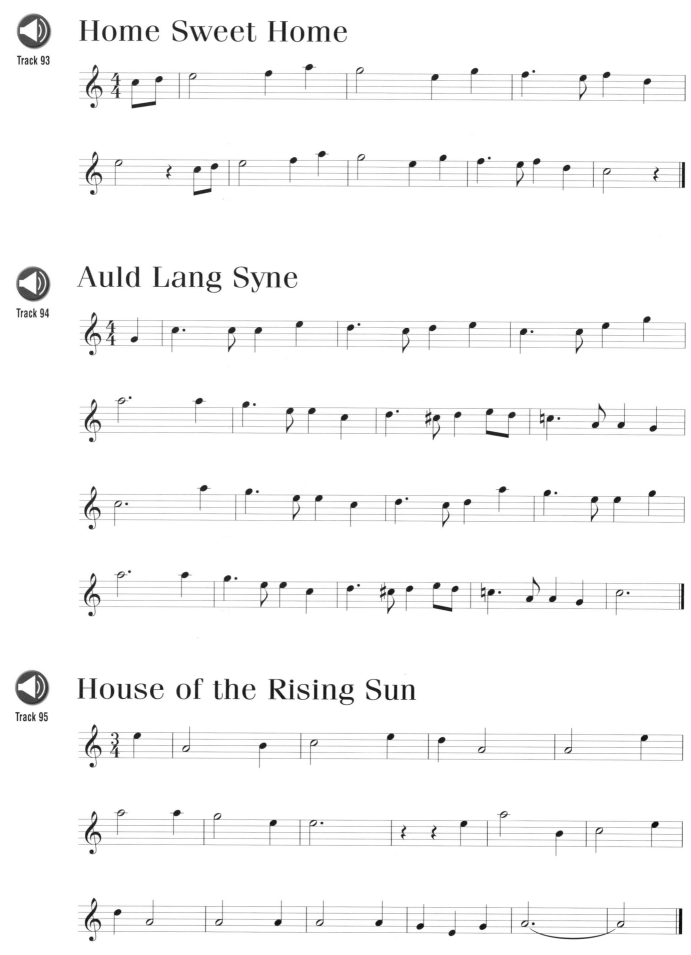

Power Chords

Track 96

Finally, let's learn one more type of chord: the **power chord**. Each of these chords uses just two strings: one open and one fretted. Also, notice that power chords are labeled with the suffix "5."

E5

■ To play the E5 chord, think: sixth string, open, and fifth string, second fret.

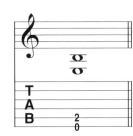

A5

■ To play the A5 chord, think: fifth string, open, and fourth string, second fret.

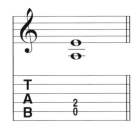

D5

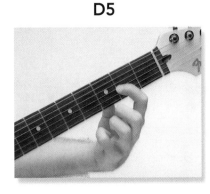

■ To play the D5 chord, think: fourth string, open, and third string, second fret.

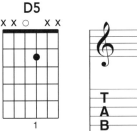

Keep It Clean

Since these chords use just two strings at a time, they don't require a full strumming motion; just enough movement to pick the two strings. To keep any upper strings from accidentally sounding when playing these chords, try letting your left-hand fretting finger lay a little bit flat, so that it touches the string(s) above lightly.

46

Warmin' Up

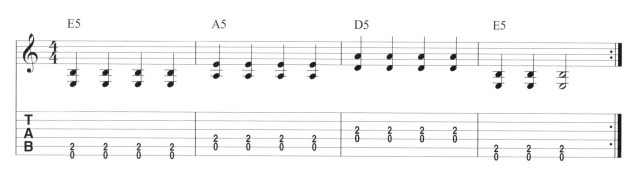

Feelin' Good

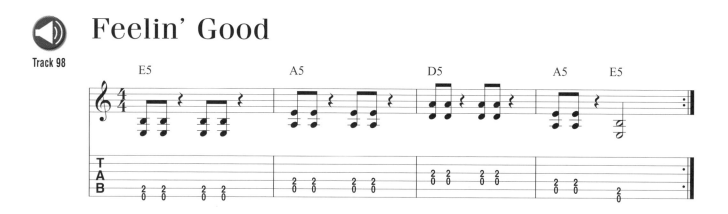

TIP: With each chord change, as you move your left hand down one string, move your right hand down one string at the same time.

Movin' and Shakin'

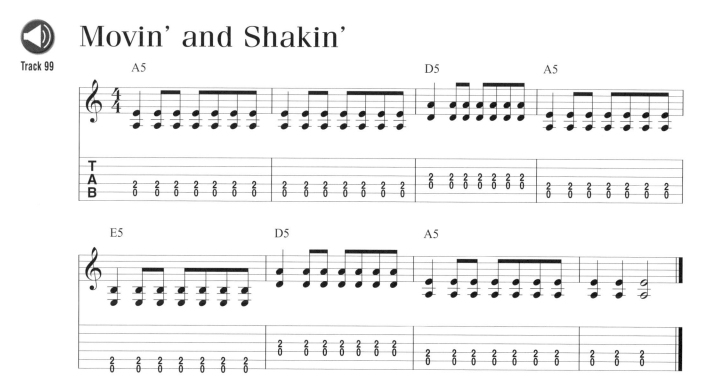

Review

Notes in First Position

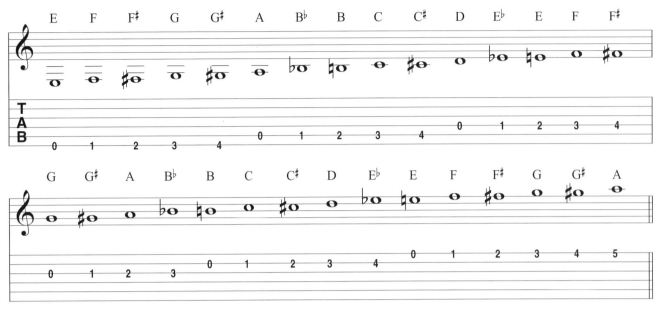

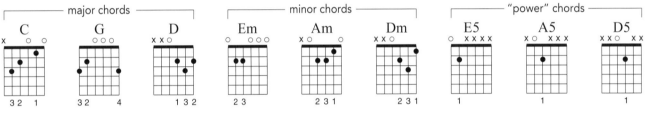

Chords

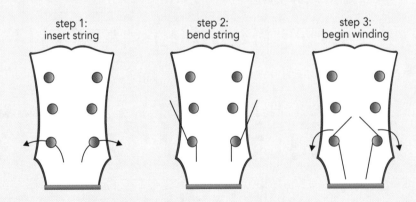

How to Change a String

If you're missing a string, or your strings are old and dirty and need replacing, you'll need to know how to change a string. The diagram below should help. Once you've inserted the string at the bridge, you need to wrap the other end around the tuning peg at the headstock. To do this, first insert the string through the posthole. Then, bend it sharply to hold the string in place, and begin winding. You should allow enough slack at the start to wrap the string completely around the peg 3-4 times, and cut off any excess when you're finished.

step 1:
insert string

step 2:
bend string

step 3:
begin winding

Keep in mind, new strings need to be "stretched out" before you can expect them to hold their pitch. You can do this by pulling on each string one at a time with your fingers (over the pickups or soundhole, away from your body) after you've strung up your guitar, then retuning each of them to the correct pitch. Repeat this until each string stays in tune even after you've pulled on it.

Movable Power Chords

Track 100

Power chords are probably the easiest type of chord to play on the guitar, and they're very common to rock and pop styles. In Lesson 12, we learned three open-position power chords: E5, A5, and D5. Now, with just one more shape, we can learn to play any power chord, anywhere along the neck...

The Two-Note Shape

This shape isn't labeled with a chord name because it's *movable*—that is, you can play it anywhere up or down the neck, and you'll get a different chord. You can base it off of the sixth string, or off of the fifth string.

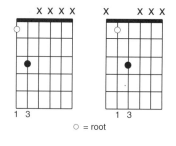

○ = root

Go ahead: pick any note along the fifth or sixth string, and apply this shape to it. The name of the power chord you're playing will always be the root (the lowest note) plus the suffix "5." For example, if you start on F, you get an F5 power chord. If you start on C, you get a C5 power chord, and so on. Here are a few examples for you to get your hands on:

▶ Notice that some power chords, like B♭5, can be played on either the 5th *or* the 6th string.

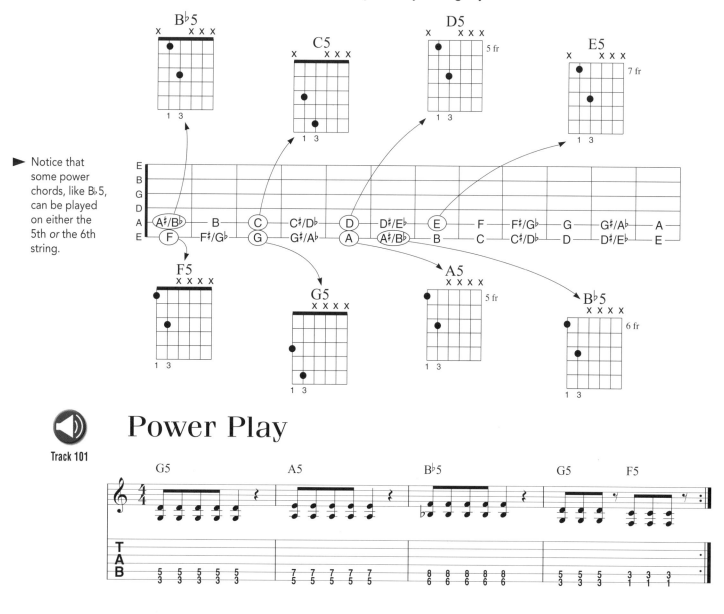

Power Play

Track 101

49

Here are a few songs that move between strings 5 and 6.

'50s Pop

Track 102

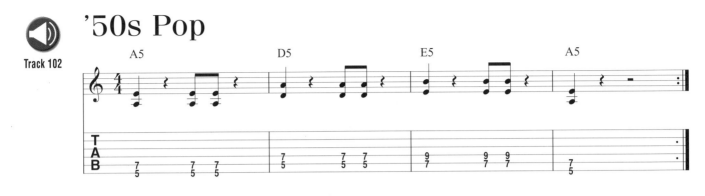

Muting the Upper Strings

To keep unwanted strings from sounding when playing power chords, let your first finger lay across the upper strings lightly. For power chords along the fifth string, allow your fingertip to mute the sixth string as well, as shown.

'60s Rock

Track 103

► To keep your left hand from cramping, try releasing it slightly as you slide from one power chord to the next.

'70s Heavy

Track 104

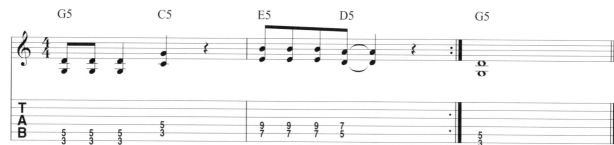

'80s Rock

Track 105

The Three-Note Shape

Just in case you're interested, here's another option for playing power chords.

This **three-note shape** sounds a little fuller than the two-note version. Otherwise, it's pretty much the same chord. You can use it anywhere along the neck, on the sixth string or the fifth string.

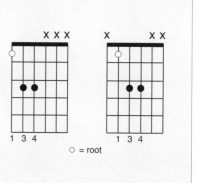

○ = root

'90s Alternative

Track 106

Palm Muting

Palm muting is a special technique in which you allow the side or heel of your picking hand to rest against the bridge, muffling or "muting" the strings as you play. Use this technique when you see the abbreviation "P.M." under the notes (between the staff and TAB).

Ridin' Down the Highway

Track 107

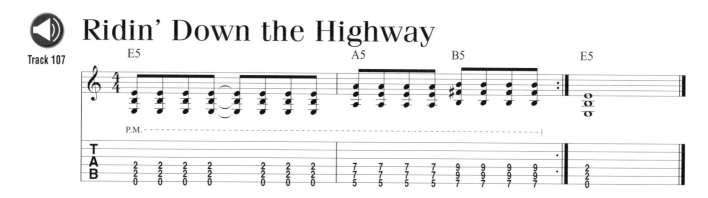

An *accent mark* (>) written above or below a note or chord means you should play that note or chord slightly louder than the others.

Thick Groove

Track 108

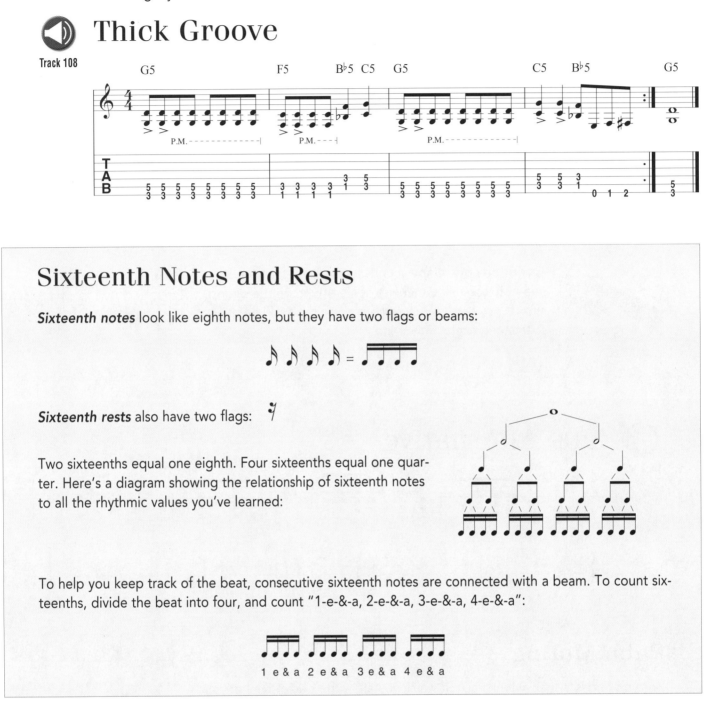

Sixteenth Notes and Rests

Sixteenth notes look like eighth notes, but they have two flags or beams:

Sixteenth rests also have two flags:

Two sixteenths equal one eighth. Four sixteenths equal one quarter. Here's a diagram showing the relationship of sixteenth notes to all the rhythmic values you've learned:

To help you keep track of the beat, consecutive sixteenth notes are connected with a beam. To count sixteenths, divide the beat into four, and count "1-e-&-a, 2-e-&-a, 3-e-&-a, 4-e-&-a":

1 e & a 2 e & a 3 e & a 4 e & a

To help you get a feel for sixteenth notes, listen to the following track, then try playing along.

Faster, Please

Track 109

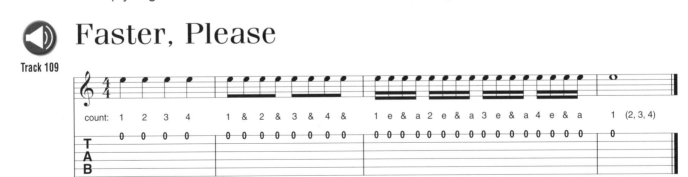

Because sixteenths move so quickly, you'll find them easier to play if you alternate down-strokes (⊓) with upstrokes (V). Try that on this example.

Alternate Sixteenths

Track 110

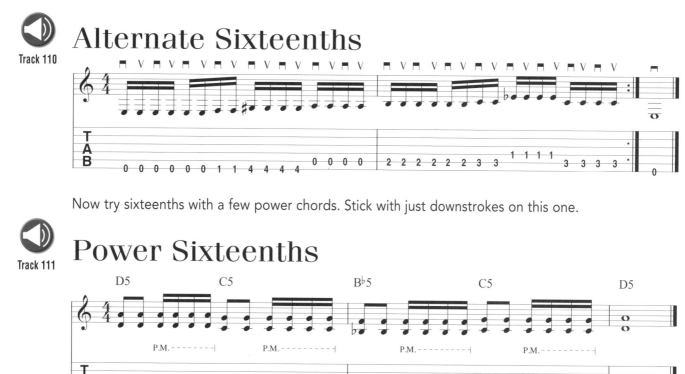

Now try sixteenths with a few power chords. Stick with just downstrokes on this one.

Power Sixteenths

Track 111

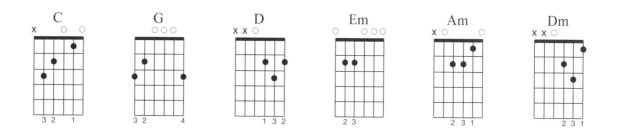

Of course, you can apply the sixteenth rhythm to open chords as well. Try alternate strumming (downstrokes and upstrokes) with these chords:

Open Chord Strumming

Track 112

▶ Tap your foot once for each quarter note, even though you're counting (and playing) in sixteenths.

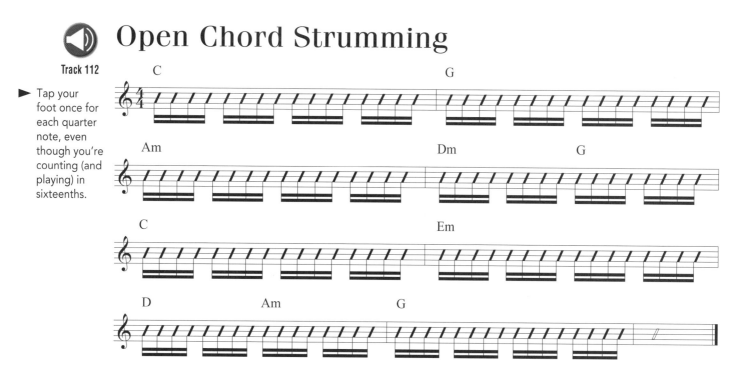

New Open Chords

Track 113

Open chords are chords that contain one or more open strings; they are the most fundamental chords to all styles of guitar playing. In Lessons 9 and 10, we learned several open chords: C, G, D, Em, Am, and Dm. Now we'll add a few more.

E

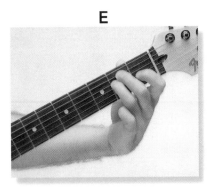

■ The open E chord is similar to Em, but you add your first finger on the third string.

A

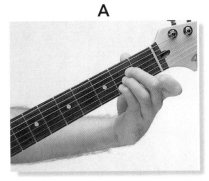

■ This open A chord is a little bit like Am, but notice that all three fingers belong on the second fret.

Try switching between E major and minor; then, between A major and minor.

Major to Minor

Track 114

Simple Strumming

Track 115

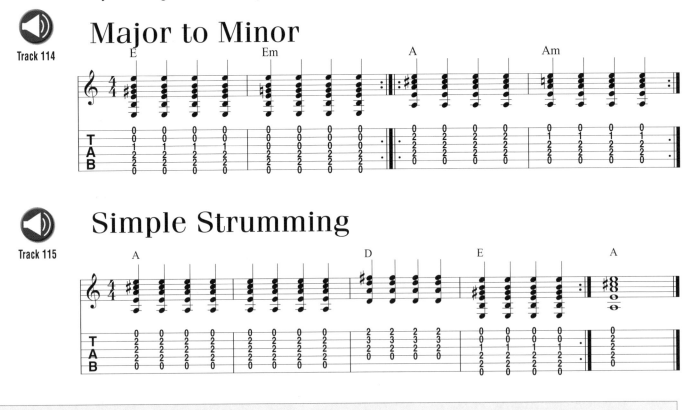

If your fingers feel too crowded on the A chord, consider an option many electric guitarists use: Flatten your first finger at the first joint, laying it across strings 2–4.

Sometimes, what chord you play isn't as important as how you play it. Let's look at a few easy strumming patterns. Play close attention to the stroke indications (⊓ and V).

Strum pattern #1

This one works great at almost any tempo.

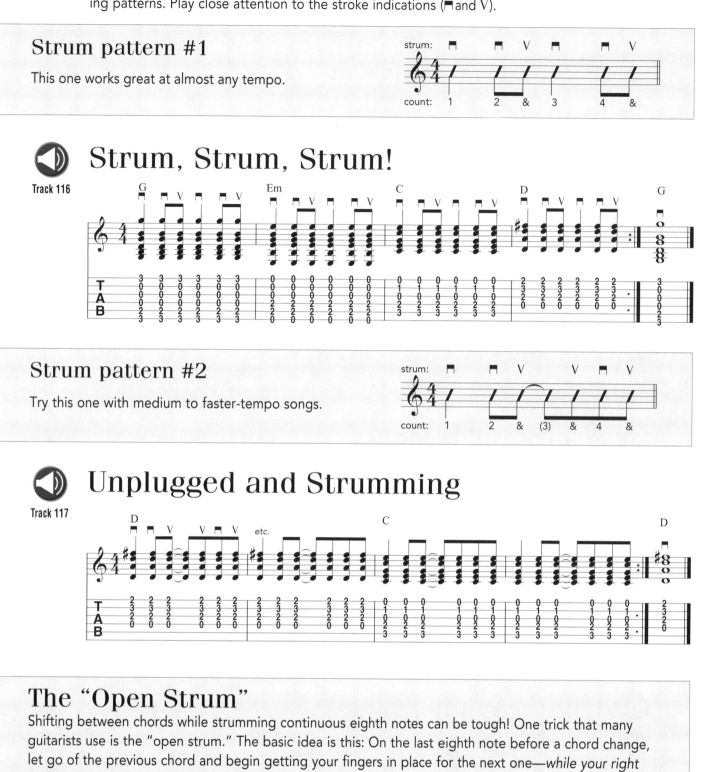

Strum, Strum, Strum!

Track 116

Strum pattern #2

Try this one with medium to faster-tempo songs.

Unplugged and Strumming

Track 117

The "Open Strum"

Shifting between chords while strumming continuous eighth notes can be tough! One trick that many guitarists use is the "open strum." The basic idea is this: On the last eighth note before a chord change, let go of the previous chord and begin getting your fingers in place for the next one—*while your right hand strums the open strings.*

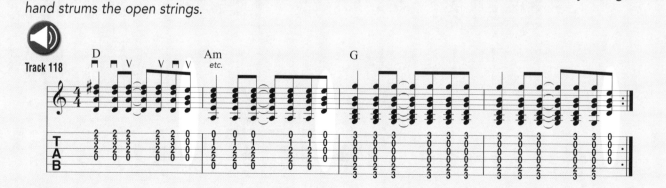

Track 118

This should give you just enough time to grab that next chord, without having to slow down or skip a beat in your strumming.

Strum pattern #3

This one uses sixteenth notes and works best with slower tempo songs.

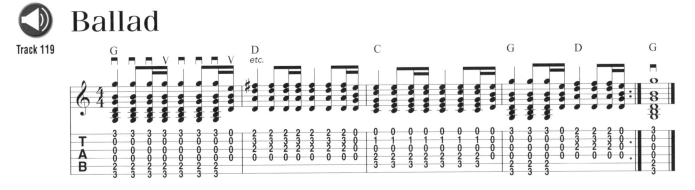

Ballad

Track 119

Strum pattern #4

Here are a few for 3/4 meter.

Waltz for Bink

Track 120

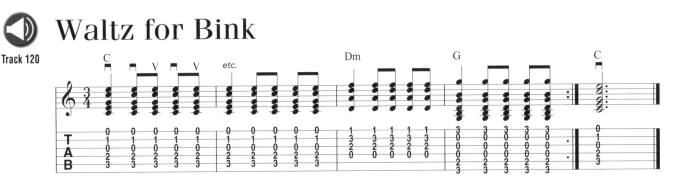

The more you play guitar, the more you'll be able to sense when to play on the beat or between beats, and when to change rhythm patterns. Notice how the strumming pattern changes from measure to measure in this next example. (Pay close attention to the downstrokes and upstrokes.)

That's What I Like

Track 121

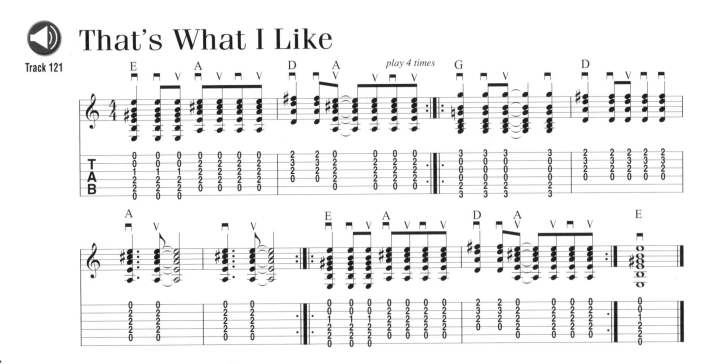

Here's another type of muting effect that can add accent and variety to your strumming patterns. Try this: while strumming a chord with your right hand, let the heel or side of your palm hit the strings a split second before you strike them with your pick. The result should be a muffled, percussive sound (indicated with an "x" in notation and TAB).

The Muted Strum

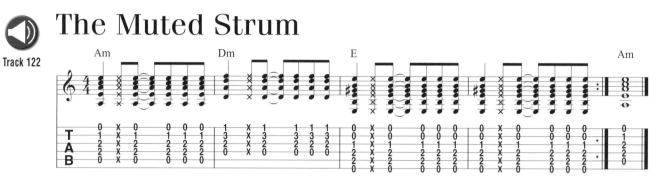

Here's a tip: With your right hand resting on the strings, the strumming motion will actually come from your wrist. It may take you a few tries to get this, so be patient. Also, don't forget to release your hand for the following upstroke!

One More Chord: F

F major requires a new technique—the use of a **barre** (pronounced "bar"). Barring is done by flattening a finger across more than one string at a time.

F

■ Flatten your first finger across strings 1 and 2, and then fret the remaining notes as shown.

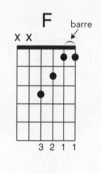

The toughest part here will be getting both notes of your barre to sound cleanly. If the chord sounds bad, play each string one at a time, then readjust your barring finger if you need to.

Country Life

Track 123

Barring comes in very handy, as we'll see later on. So practice this technique until it comes naturally.

The Shape of Things to Come

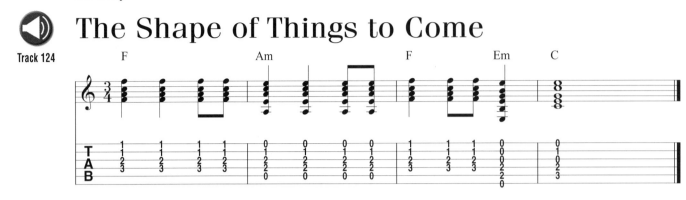

Arpeggios (a.k.a. Broken Chords)

Strumming isn't your only option when playing chords; another way to play chords is by picking them, one note at a time. *Arpeggios* (or *broken chords*) offer a lighter accompanimental approach. They work nicely for ballads—or just about any style, really.

Track 125

One advantage of arpeggios is that they give you more time to fret each chord—technically, you only need to lay down one finger at a time.

Note by Note

Track 126

► Once each finger is in place, hold it there for the duration of the chord.

LESSON 15

First Position Review

Track 127

Let's take some time to review the notes that we learned in Book 1. This area of the guitar neck is known as *first position*.

Notice that some frets seem to have two different note names, like F♯ and G♭? These are called *enharmonic equivalents*—two different note names for the same pitch. Either spelling is acceptable.

first position

E	F	F♯/G♭	G	G♯/A♭	A
B	C	C♯/D♭	D	D♯/E♭	
G	G♯/A♭	A	A♯/B♭	B	
D	D♯/E♭	E	F	F♯/G♭	
A	A♯/B♭	B	C	C♯/D♭	
E	F	F♯/G♭	G	G♯/A♭	

*This note can also be played on the third string, fourth fret.

Remember: in general, we follow the *one-finger-per-fret* rule—first finger on the first fret, second finger on the second fret, and so on. The exception is the high A, which can be played by sliding the pinky up to the fifth fret.

The Road to Glory

Track 128

Syncopation

Track 129

► Playing notes "off the beat" is a way of adding rhythmic interest to a melody or riff.

This song has a **1st and 2nd ending** (indicated by brackets and the numbers "1" and "2"). When you finish the 1st ending, return to the initial repeat sign (|:) and continue. The second time through, skip the 1st ending and jump to the 2nd ending, playing until the end of the song.

Star-Spangled Banner

Track 130

▶ A *fermata* sign (⌢) tells you to hold a note for longer than its full value.

Think Chordally!

Sometimes, a melody will force you to stray from the one-finger-per-fret rule—for instance, if there are two notes, one right after another, on different strings but the same fret. In order to play such a line smoothly and connectedly, you'll need to use a more creative fingering.

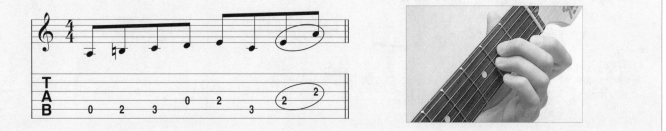

60

In the Hall of the Mountain King

Track 131

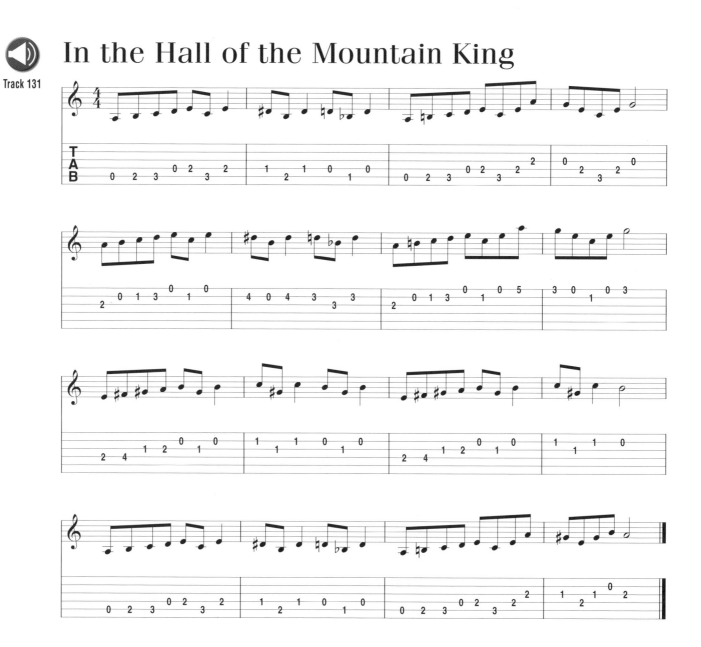

In some songs, it's common to see the instruction "***let ring.***" This simply means that, instead of releasing your fingers after each note is played, you hold them down, allowing the notes to sustain.

Estudio

Track 132

Scales and Keys

Track 133

Now that you've begun to get a handle on the basic materials of music—notes and chords—it's time to start looking at how music is organized. Let's take a look at two very important concepts in music: *scale* and *key*.

What's a Scale?

A scale is a series of notes used to create a melody, a solo, or a lick. Two things give a scale its name: the scale's **root** (the lowest note), and its **quality**, which is determined by the pattern of whole steps and half steps it follows.

Here's a look at the two most important scale qualities:

The Major Scale

The root note here is C, and the quality is major, so this is a C major scale.

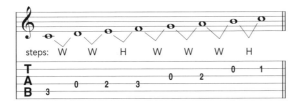

The Minor Scale

The root here is C, but the pattern of whole and half steps makes it a C minor scale.

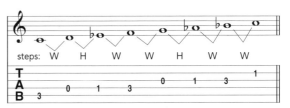

Remember: from one fret to the next on your guitar equals one half step (H); two frets equal a whole step (W).

What's a Key?

When we see that a the notes of a particular song come from a certain scale, we say that the song is *in the key of* that scale. For instance, if the notes of a song all come from the C major scale, we say that the song is in the key of C major.

Try playing through the above C major scale, but change the order of the notes. Begin and end your improvisation on the note C. Notice how the scale seems to be "at rest" when you arrive at C? This is because the note C is the root, or **tonic**—the note around which the key revolves.

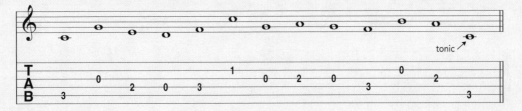

Most scales and keys—except for C major and A minor—contain sharped or flatted notes. Instead of writing these out as they occur, a **key signature** is used at the beginning of each line of music to tell you:

- What notes should be played sharp or flat throughout a song.
- The song's key

For example, the key of G major contains F♯, so its key signature will have or sharp on the F-line. This tells you to play all Fs as F♯ (unless, of course, you see a natural sign ♮.)

key signature

Let's look at some common *major* scales and keys...

Key of C

Based on the C major scale, which has no sharps or flats:

Simple Gifts

Track 134

► "Simple Gifts" is in the key of C; the notes in the song all come from the C major scale.

Key of G

Based on the G major scale, which has one sharp, F♯:

Jamaica Farewell

Track 135

Key of F

Based on the F major scale, which has one flat, B♭ :

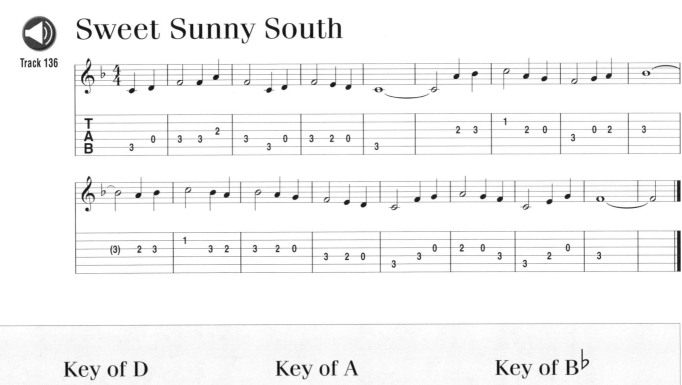

Sweet Sunny South

Track 136

| Key of D | Key of A | Key of B♭ |

Transposition

Track 137

Sometimes, you'll find a song that's written either too high or too low for you to sing or play. The solution is to play the song in a different key—one that's more comfortable. Changing the key of a song like this is called *transposition*. Try playing the following simple tune—"Yankee Doodle"— in the keys below. The transposition has already been done for you.

New Chords: Dominant 7ths

Keys can also be defined by the chords of a song, and one of the most tell-tale chords is the dominant seventh. Get your fingers on these dominant seventh chords and listen to their sound.

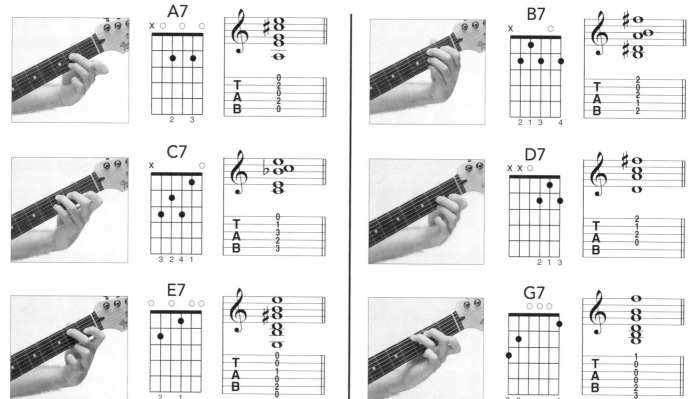

Notice how these chords sound "unresolved?" A dominant chord adds a bit of musical "tension" and makes the ear want "relief." This relief can come from a major or minor chord played after the dominant chord, as in this example:

Seventh Heaven

Track 138

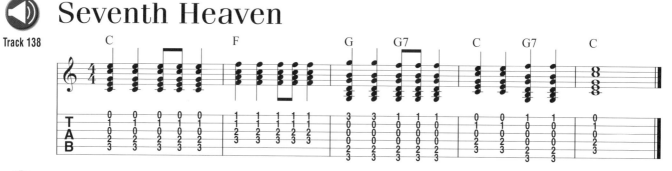

Bluesy Sevenths

Track 139

▶ Some songs sort of "leave you hanging" by never resolving the dominant chord.

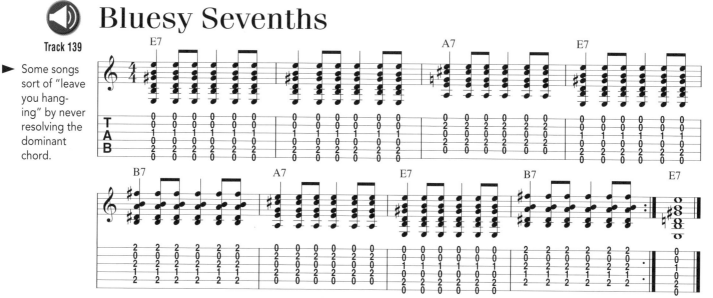

The Blues

Track 140

There are many different styles of music—rock, pop, country, classical, jazz, and so on. Blues is one style of music that's very popular, and it's fun to learn. What is *blues*? Well, like any style, blues is characterized by the chords, progressions, and scales it uses, as well as what forms they all fit into.

The I, IV, and V Chords

Generally, blues songs use only three chords: the first, fourth, and fifth chords of the key (indicated with Roman numerals I, IV, and V). To find these chords, count up the scale from the root of the key:

Key	Chord / Scale Tone							
	I			**IV**	**V**			
Blues in "C"	C	D	E	F	G	A	B	C
Blues in "F"	F	G	A	B♭	C	D	E	F
Blues in "G"	G	A	B	C	D	E	F♯	G
Blues in "D"	D	E	F♯	G	A	B	C♯	D
Blues in "A"	A	B	C♯	D	E	F♯	G♯	A
Blues in "E"	E	F♯	G♯	A	B	C♯	D♯	E

The I, IV, and V chords are actually common to all styles of music (so get to know them!). Often, the V chord is played as a dominant seventh chord—like G7, C7, D7, etc.—instead of as a major chord.

The 12-Bar Form

Part of what makes blues unique is that it uses the I, IV, and V chords in a very predictable sequence. The most common is the 12-bar form. This doesn't mean that the song is only 12 bars (or measures) long. Rather, it uses one or more 12-bar phrases, which repeat over and over.

Track 141

► Remember *slash notation*? It tells you how many beats each chord is played. Vary your strum patterns.

Blues in C

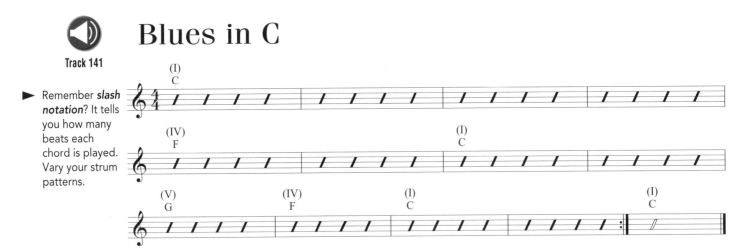

Notice the number of measures that each chord is played. This is the most common 12-bar blues progression. It can be transposed to any key, and it will still sound like the blues.

The last two measures of the 12-bar form are sometimes called the **turnaround**—since they "turn" the form back "around" to the beginning. Musicians sometimes vary the **turnaround**, using different chords or even a riff.

The most common variation is to add a V chord in the very last measure:

Blues in G

Track 142

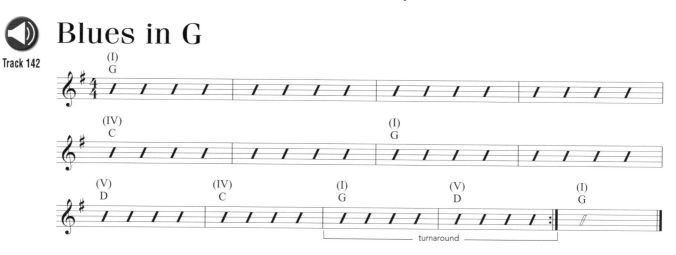

Minor chords are also very popular in blues progressions. This track has a "rock" feel.

Minor Blues

Track 143

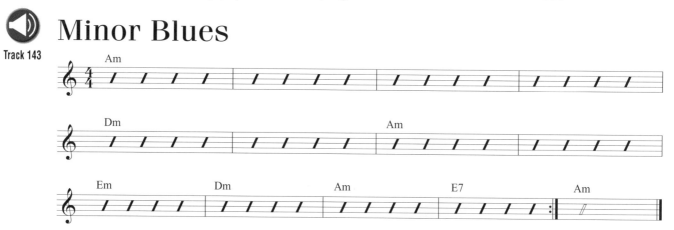

The use of all dominant sevenths is another option unique to the blues. (In most other styles, the dominant seventh is reserved for the V chord only.)

Seventh Chord Blues

Track 144

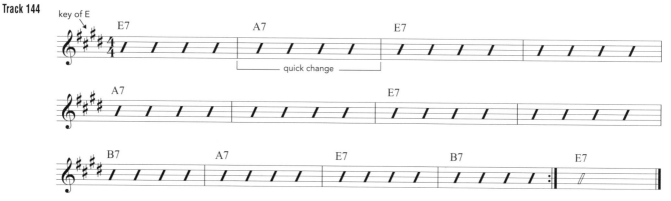

See the IV chord in measure 2? This is called a **quick change**, since you "change" to the IV and "quickly" return to the I.

Blues progressions don't necessarily require full chords. The following blues-based "back and forth" rhythm was made popular by Chuck Berry and other early rock 'n' roll players.

Berry Pickin'

Track 145

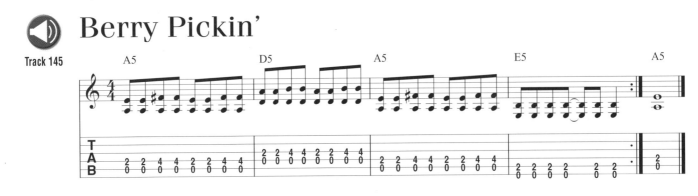

Moving Up the Neck

The "back-and-forth" rhythm can be applied to movable power chords fairly easily. First, play a two-note movable power chord, then keep your fingers in the same shape and add your pinky two frets above your third finger. You may feel a bit of a stretch, but hang in there.

Rockin' Blues

Track 146

► Also try playing the power chord with your first and second fingers instead, adding your pinky for the top note.

The Blues Scale

If you want to spice up a blues jam, try soloing over a 12-bar section using notes from the blues scale. This scale is actually popular in rock and jazz as well. First, notice the scale's step pattern, then learn its fingering.

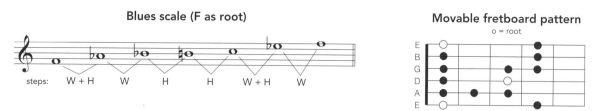

Blues scale (F as root)

Movable fretboard pattern

o = root

steps: W + H   W   H   H   W + H   W

As with the major and minor scales you learned, the blues scale can be started from any root note. Plus, this particular fretboard pattern is movable—meaning that you can slide it up the neck and start it from any root along the sixth string. Commit it to memory, and use it to form some great riffs and solos like this one:

Track 147

Takin' the Lea

Introducing... The Shuffle Feel

The **shuffle feel** is a very common element of rock, blues, pop, and jazz music. It uses a new rhythmic value called a triplet.

By now, you know that a quarter note divided into two equal parts is two eighth notes. And a quarter note divided into four equal parts is four sixteenth notes. But a quarter note divided into three equal parts? This is an **eighth-note triplet**:

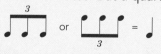

Triplets are beamed together with a number 3. To count a triplet, simply say the word "tri-pl-et" during one beat. Tap your foot to the beat, and count out loud:

count: 1   2   tri - pl - let   4   tri - pl - let   tri - pl - let   3   4   1   2   & tri - pl - let   4

Shuffle rhythm can be derived from a triplet rhythm by inserting a rest in the middle of the triplet, or by combining the first two eighth notes of the triplet into a quarter. The result is like a triplet with a silent middle eighth note.

Once you get a hang of this "bouncy" feel, you'll never forget it...

Chuck's Blues

Track 148

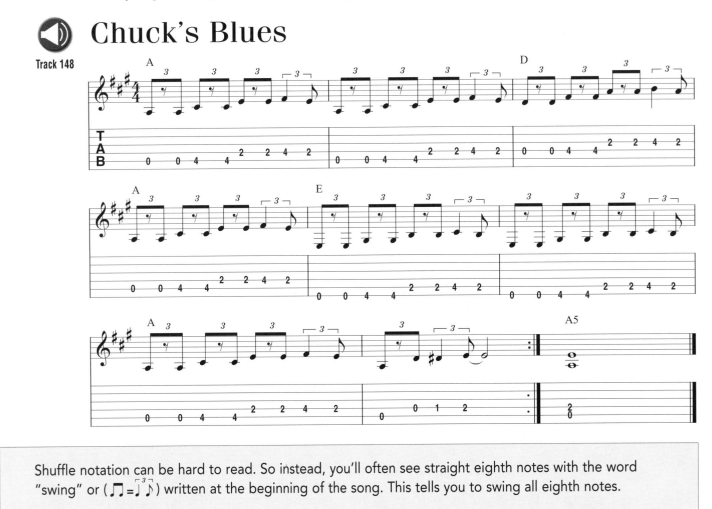

Shuffle notation can be hard to read. So instead, you'll often see straight eighth notes with the word "swing" or (♫ = ♩ ♪) written at the beginning of the song. This tells you to swing all eighth notes.

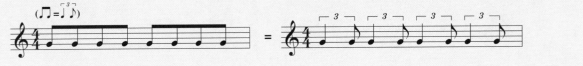

Blue Note Shuffle

Track 149

The Fifth Position

Track 150

So far, we've learned to read in the first position of the guitar—a skill that will serve us well in many situations and in many styles of music. But not every song can be played down there, so let's move on up to the *fifth position*.

Fifth position starts on the high A at the 5th fret—this time played with the index finger. (Most guitars have a white dot, or other marker, at the 5th fret, which should help you find this position quickly.)

Starting at the 5th fret allows us to access several more notes on the high E string that weren't available to us in first position. Of course, it also gives new fingerings for many familiar notes. Take a few minutes to review the diagram and exercise below.

			A	A♯/B♭	B	C	C♯/D♭
E			E	F	F♯/G♭	G	G♯/A♭
B			C	C♯/D♭	D	D♯/E♭	
G			G	G♯/A♭	A	A♯/B♭	B
D			D	D♯/E♭	E	F	F♯/G♭
A			A	A♯/B♭	B	C	C♯/D♭

frets: 3   5   7   9

You may notice that, since we no longer have the open strings working for us, we have to cover more frets—in general, follow the one-finger-per-fret rule, but allow your pinky to fret both the 8th and 9th frets.

Fifth Position

► Make sure you spend time learning where the notes are both on the fretboard *and* on the staff. (Tell your fingers what you're play-ing—say each note aloud as you play it.)

*This note can also be played at the third string, fourth fret.

To give you a better feel for this position, try a few scales. This one can be played in open posi-tion or fifth, so try it both ways.

Track 151

A Minor

C Major

▶ This one takes advantage of new high notes on the first string.

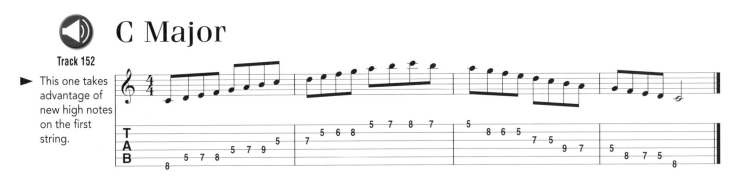

Next, try some riffs in this new position.

Hazy Days

Blue House

▶ This one uses some open strings (the low E and A) while your left hand stays in fifth position.

Another One

You can use almost any of the songs in the first half of the book to practice playing in 5th position, and this is probably the best way to really learn it. (Go ahead—the time you spend will be well worth it.)

When you think you know this position well enough, try some new songs, like these:

Drunken Sailor

Track 156

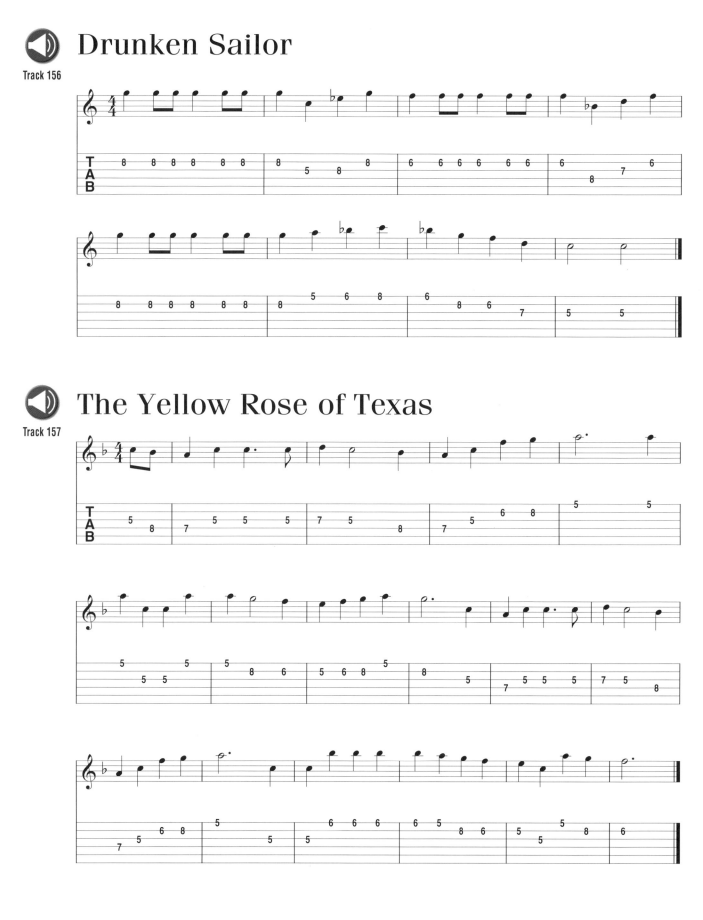

The Yellow Rose of Texas

Track 157

Take it slow and easy.

Shenandoah

Changing Positions

Sometimes, you'll want to use more than one position to play a song—for instance, you might start a song in open position, then move up to fifth position for some higher notes, then move back down again. If you don't have TAB to show you the convenient positions, it's a good idea to survey the song before playing it, and mark the appropriate spots to change positions. Use Roman numerals (I and V) to mark these position changes.

Arkansas Traveler

► If your strings "squeak" a bit as you move between positions, don't worry about it; try releasing your left-hand pressure as you move between positions.

Rock-a-Bye

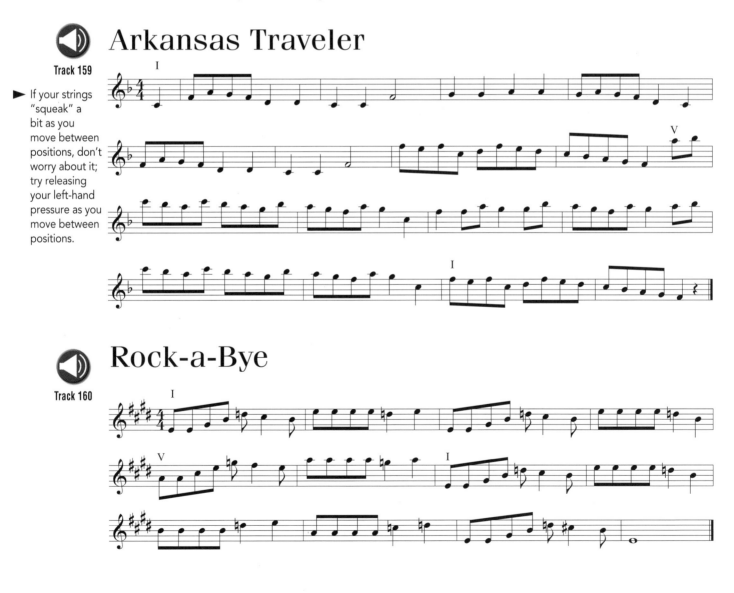

Barre Chords

Remember the barre technique we used in playing the F chord? This is actually a very common tool in guitar playing. In fact, we use it to form **movable barre chords**—major and minor chords that can be played anywhere along the neck using just a few simple shapes.

We'll learn four types of barre chords, based on four different open position chords: E, Em, A, and Am. But first, let's work on that barre. WARNING: This may be the most difficult technique you undertake as a beginning guitarist! The key to your ultimate success will be practice and patience.

The Full Barre

barre symbol

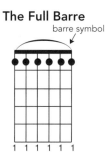

The Full Barre

The real trick to playing barre chords is being able to barre across all six strings of the guitar with just your index finger—*and* have each string sound clearly. So let's practice this first:

Step 1: Form a full barre by flattening your first finger across all six strings. Try this at the first fret.

Step 2: Support the barre by placing your thumb on the underside of the guitar neck, directly beneath your first finger. (Think of the thumb and index finger as a clamp that presses the neck together.)

Step 3: Strum all six strings. Readjust your finger, if necessary, until every string sounds clearly. HINT: It usually helps to turn your first finger slightly to the side when using it to barre.

The "Eight-Barre" Blues

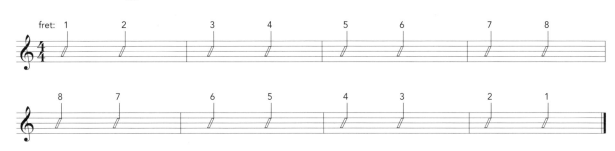

E-Type Barre Chord

The first form that we'll learn is called the E-type barre chord, because it looks like an E chord. We'll use this E shape to play major chords up and down the sixth string.

E

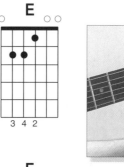

Step 1: Play an open E major chord, but use your 2nd, 3rd, and 4th fingers. (That's right, this is a new fingering.)

3 4 2

F

Step 2: Slide this chord shape up one fret, and add your 1st finger across the 1st fret, forming a barre.

1 3 4 2 1 1

Now, just strum all six strings, and voilà—your first barre chord! This particular barre chord is F major because its root is F on the sixth string. But you can apply this same shape to any root note along the sixth string:

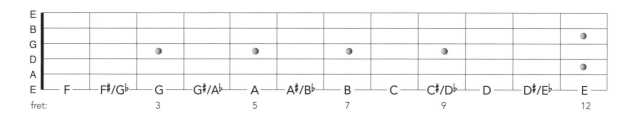

Most guitars have mother-of-pearl inlay markers on the fretboard to make it easier for you to find positions. The third, fifth, seventh, and ninth frets are commonly marked with a single inlay, while the twelfth fret is usually marked with a double inlay to indicate the octave position.

Sweet Mother of Pearl!

Track 163

Let's try some riffs that move this shape around.

Life's Good

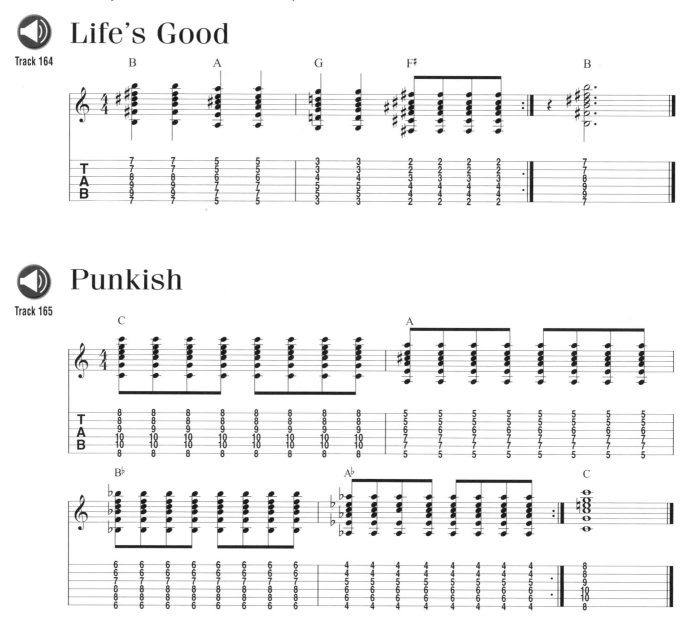

Track 164

Punkish

Track 165

The "Thumb-and-Index" Barre

If you just can't get that index finger to barre across all six strings, here's a quick-and-dirty shortcut: Let your index finger barre just the top two strings, and allow your thumb to wrap around the top of the neck, fretting the sixth string. This works especially well on electric guitars.

WARNING: Even if you can do this alternate barre, don't stop working on your full barre! You'll be glad you did.

The Staccato Effect

Some songs are played with a short, bouncy articulation called staccato. This is indicated by a dot above the note or chord.

Track 166

To produce this sound, first play the chord as normal, then quickly release your left-hand pressure without losing contact with the strings.

The Percussion Effect, a.k.a. "Chord Scratch"

Taking this one step further, try strumming the strings while your left hand rests lightly against them. You should get a muted, percussive sound—indicated by an "x" in notation and TAB.

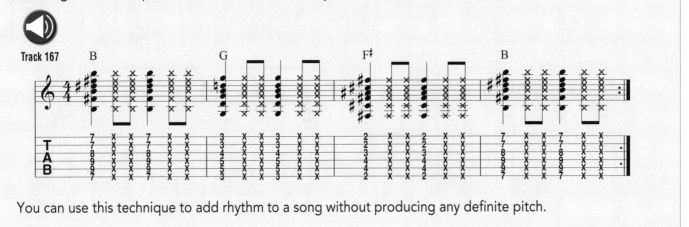

Track 167

You can use this technique to add rhythm to a song without producing any definite pitch.

The Way I Feel

Track 168

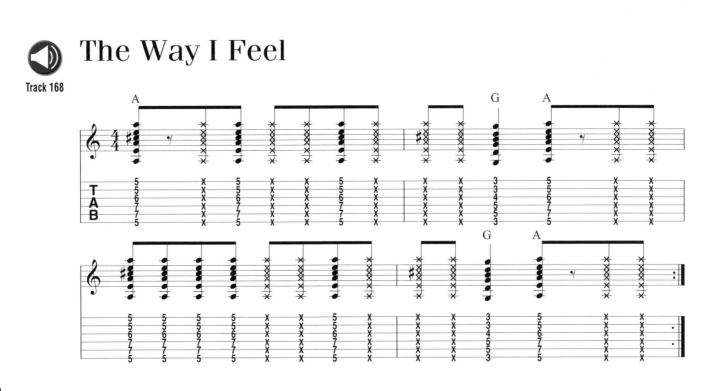

Em-Type Barre Chord

The same barring technique can be used for minor chords too. Since we used the E major shape for the major barre chords, we'll use the E minor shape for the minor barre chords along the sixth string.

Step 1: Play an open Em chord, using your 3rd and 4th fingers.

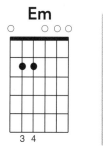

Step 2: Slide the Em shape up one fret, and add a 1st finger barre across the 1st fret.

Voilà—an Fm barre chord! Now try switching between your major and minor barre chords. It's as easy as lifting a finger.

From Major to Minor

Track 169

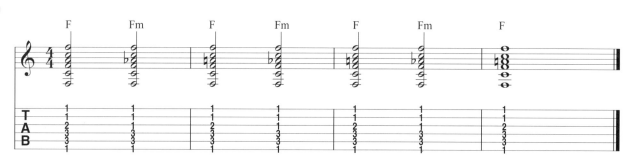

Minor Vamp

Track 170

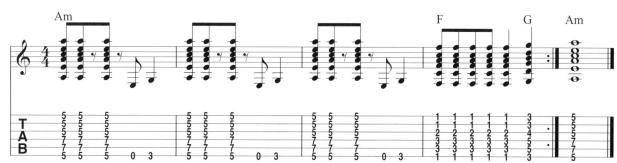

79

Choosing the Best Chord Position

Although you should learn to play barre chords in all positions, in actual music, you'll often want to mix barre chords with open-position chords. Not only is this easier on the left hand, it adds more variety to your sound.

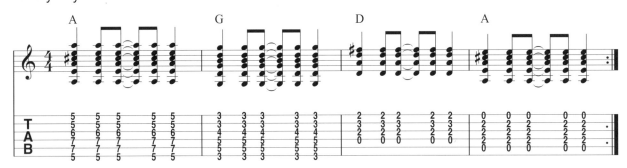

Some progressions are impossible to play without barre chords:

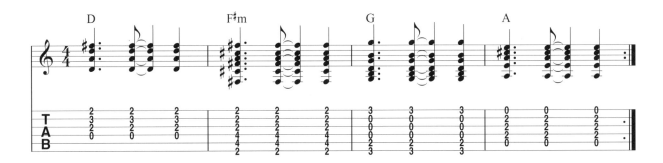

Others just sound better when played with barre chords:

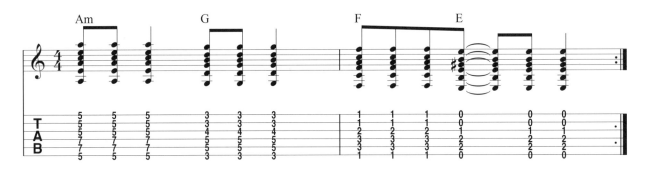

Still Having Trouble?

The easiest barre chords to play are those at the area of the fifth fret. However, with practice, your hand will become stronger, and you'll have less difficulty playing barre chords in any position. In the meantime, remember the following:

- Use just enough pressure on the strings to produce a clear tone.

- Always place your left thumb on the guitar neck *directly behind the barre* for additional support.

- When moving from one barre chord to another, keep your fingers in position and release pressure slightly, without losing contact with the strings.

Just as we converted the E and Em chord shapes into barre chords, we can do the same with A and Am chord shapes. These will have their roots on the fifth string.

A-Type Barre Chord

The formula is essentially the same: start with an open A chord, then move it up one fret and add a first-finger barre.

Open A chord shape...   ...converted barre chord shape

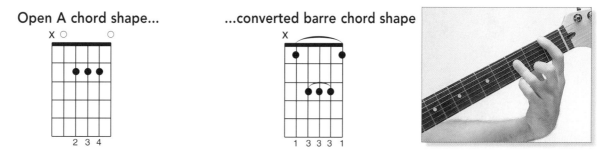

Instead of fretting each note individually for the A shape, try forming another barre with your third finger, as shown. Bend your third finger at the knuckle and lay it across strings 2-4. Once you get used to it, this fingering is a lot easier to move up and down the neck.

Am-Type Barre Chord

Once again: start with an open Am, move it up a fret and add the first-finger barre. Notice how this looks like the "E" type barre chord but moved over one string?

Open Am chord shape...   ...converted barre chord shape

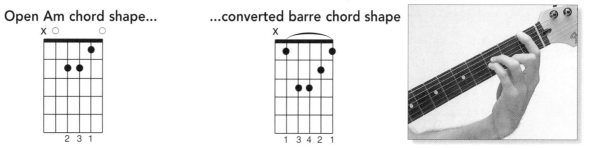

Practice these A-form barre chords up and down the neck. Remember: the root of these shapes lies along the fifth string:

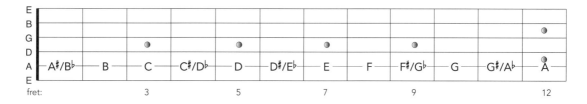

Strollin'

Track 172

► Be patient; barre chords can take weeks or even months of practice.

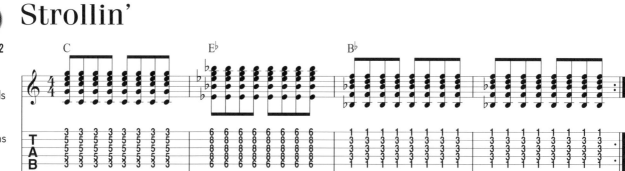

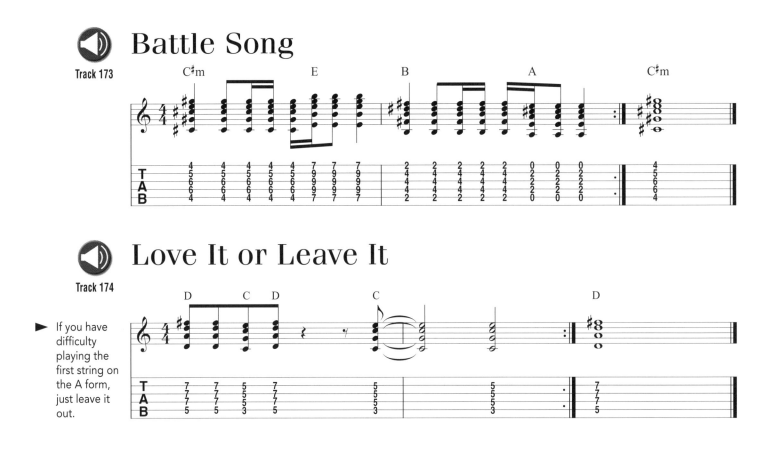

Battle Song

Track 173

Love It or Leave It

Track 174

► If you have difficulty playing the first string on the A form, just leave it out.

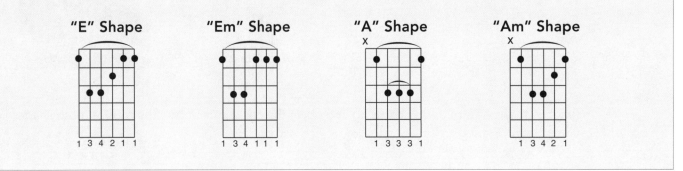

Four Shapes In All

It shouldn't take much movement to shift from E-form to A-form barre chords. The first finger can remain in place; then it's just a matter of moving fingers 2-4, or rolling the third finger into place.

"E" Shape

1 3 4 2 1 1

"Em" Shape

1 3 4 1 1 1

"A" Shape
x

1 3 3 3 1

"Am" Shape
x

1 3 4 2 1

Song 1

Track 175

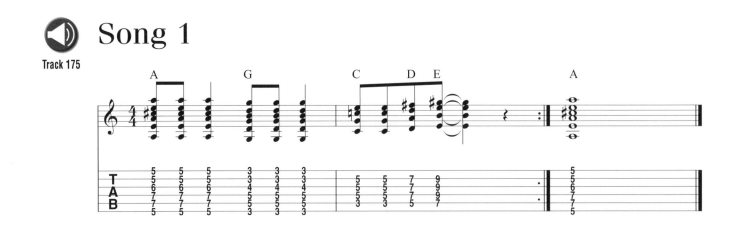

Tango

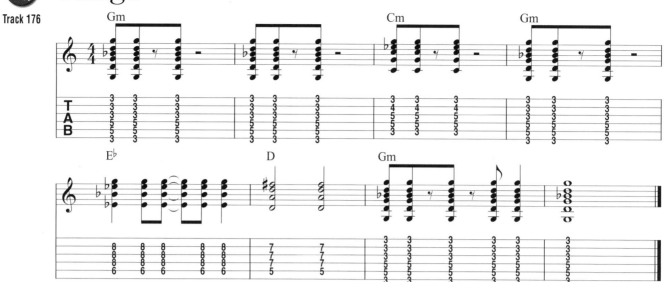

Feelin' Good

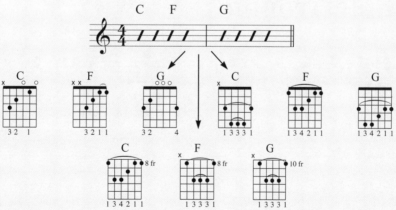

Choosing the Best Chord Position, Pt. 2

Using combinations of E-form and A-form barre chords—as well as open-position chords—can help you avoid large position jumps in your playing. For example, this chord progression could be played at least three ways:

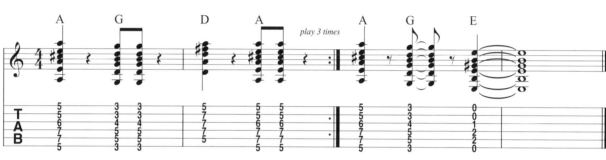

Before learning a song, play through the arrangement and select:

- the chords that sound best for each measure—open or barre.
- the chords that give you enough time to change positions.

When you have a choice of positions for the same chord:

- Use a chord position on a higher fret to produce a sharper, thinner sound.
- Use a chord position on a lower fret to produce a heavier, fuller sound.

Slides, Hammer-Ons, Pull-Offs, and Bends

LESSON 20

Track 178

Sometimes, it's not so much what you play, it's how you play it. In music terms, this is called *articulation*. Slides, hammer-ons, pull-offs, and bends all belong to a special category of articulations called *legato*. Legato techniques allows you to "slur" two or more notes together to create a smooth, flowing sound.

With all of these techniques, you'll be playing one note as you normally would—with a pick held in your right hand. But the next note (the slurred one), you'll be articulating with your left hand only.

Slides

Pick the first note, then sound the second note by sliding the same left-hand finger up or down along the string. (The second note is not picked.)

The best way to practice this is in some riffs.

Track 179

► Use your first and third fingers for this first riff. (Your third finger will do the sliding.)

Smooth

Track 180

► Use an index-finger barre, or your ring and pinky fingers together, for this slide.

Double Trouble

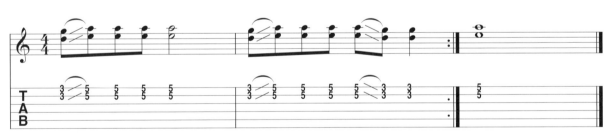

Track 181

Slidin' Power

Hammer-Ons

Pick the first note, then tap, or "hammer on," to the higher note with another left-hand finger, along the same string. If you hammer too hard, your fingertips will hurt; too soft, and you won't hear anything. Keep practicing until you think you've got it.

Track 182

Work It Out

Long Long Ago

Track 183

► Hammer-ons can work for chords as well.

Pull-Offs

A pull-off is the opposite of a hammer-on. First, start with both fingers planted. Pick the higher note, then tug or "pull" that finger off the string to sound the lower note, already fretted by the lower finger.

Back and Forth

Track 184

Push and Pull

Track 185

At the Roadhouse

Track 186

► Hammer-ons and pull-offs together make a popular combination.

Bends

In general, bending is done on the first three strings, bending "up," or towards the ceiling. Most bends are either whole-step or half-step.

Whole-step bend

Pick the note indicated (D), then push the string upwards until it matches the sound of the target pitch (E), one whole step higher. (To check yourself, play E on fret 9 first.)

Half-step bend

Pick the note indicated (D), then push the string upwards, but not quite as high, to match the target pitch (E♭) one half step higher. (Check yourself with fret 8.)

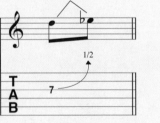

Bends are usually easiest when done with the third finger. For more strength and support, allow your first and second fingers to back up the third finger. This is called *reinforced bending*.

Bendin' Up

Track 187

► To get more leverage, don't forget to push down with your thumb on the back of the neck.

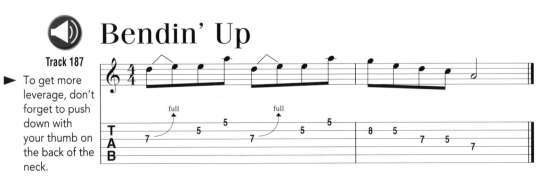

Up and Down

Track 188

► Once you've bent up, you may as well bring it back down.

Double Stops

Track 189

► Use your third and fourth fingers together for this double bend.

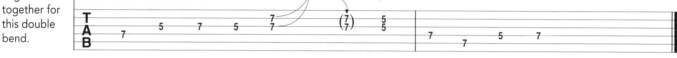

Of course, slides, hammer-ons, pull-offs, and bends can all be combined for some really cool licks.

Riff-a-Rama

Track 190

Grace-note bends differ from the other bends only in their rhythm—the first note (the one being bent) does not take up any time. Strike the first note (the grace note) with your pick, then immediately bend it upward to the next note.

Odds 'n' Ends

Minor Scales & Keys

Track 191

As we mentioned previously, music can be based in both major and minor keys. Here are a few of the most commonly used minor scales:

Key of A minor

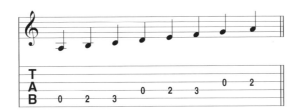

Key of E minor

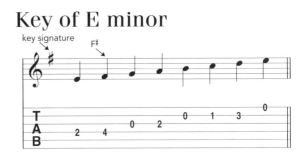

Key of D minor

Notice anything familar about these key signatures? They're the same ones that we learned for C major, G major, and F major! That's because each of these is a *relative minor* of a major scale—containing the same notes, just played in a different order, with a different emphasis.

Am Riff

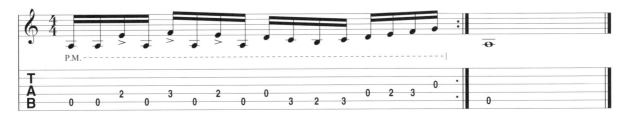

Em Riff

Dm Riff

88

The I, IV, and V chords are important in all keys—including minor ones. However, in minor keys, these chords are typically minor (indicated with lower-case Roman numerals i, iv, v)—except for the "five" chord, which can be major (V) or dominant (V7).

Key	Chord / Scale Tone							
	i			**iv**	**v or V**			
A minor	Am	B	C	Dm	Em or E	F	G	A
D minor	Dm	E	F	Gm	Am or A	B♭	C	D
E minor	Em	F♯	G	Am	Bm or B	C	D	E

i-iv-V

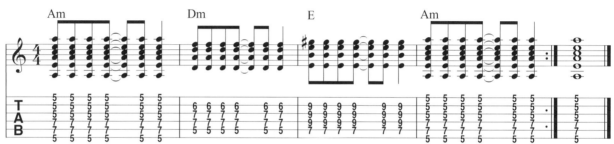

Just because i, iv, and V are important doesn't mean you can't use other chords.

Other Chords

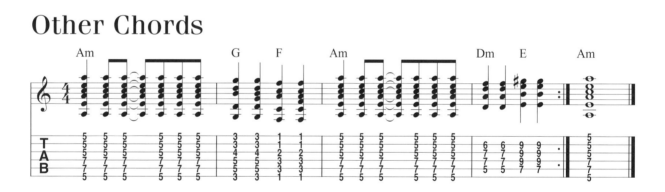

The Circle of Fifths

The **circle of fifths** is a useful tool if you want to know what chords are available within a key. Major keys line the ouside of the circle; their relative minors line the inside.

Right now, the box is highlighting chords that belong to both C major and its relative A minor—that is, F, C, G, Dm, Am, Em. To find the chords for another key, just mentally rotate the box.

For example, if a song contains the chords D, A, E, and Bm, what key is it in?

Answer: A major!

Dominant Seventh Barre Chords

Track 192

Here are a few barre chord voicings for dominant sevenths. The E7-type works anywhere along the sixth string; the A7-type, anywhere along the fifth string.

Open E7 chord shape...

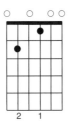

...converted barre chord shape

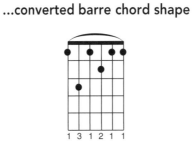

Open A7 chord shape...

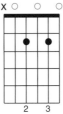

...converted barre chord shape

Mustang Sarah

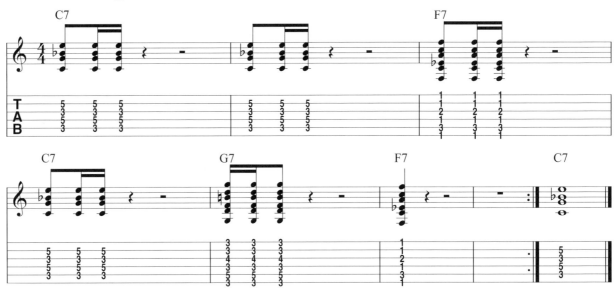

How Sweet It Is

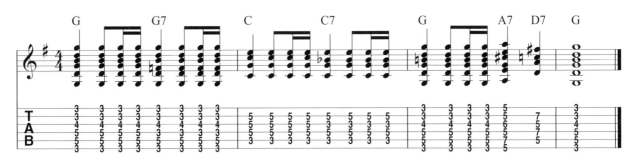

90

Movable Scale Forms

Track 193

Like power chords and barre chords, scales are easier to use if they are movable—that way, a few shapes moved up and down the neck allow you to play in any key. We already learned one movable scale form—the "blues" scale; here are two more essential patterns:

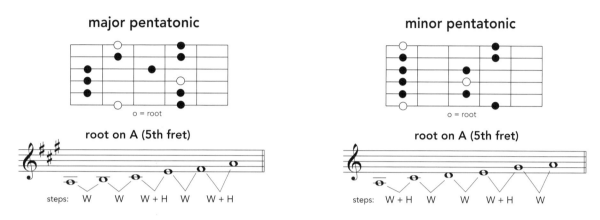

These are actually just simplified versions of the major and minor scales we already learned, with just five notes in each octave instead of seven. (The prefix **penta-** means "five.") With fewer notes, these scales have a smoother, more streamlined sound, making them especially good for improvising.

Major Pentatonic

Minor Pentatonic

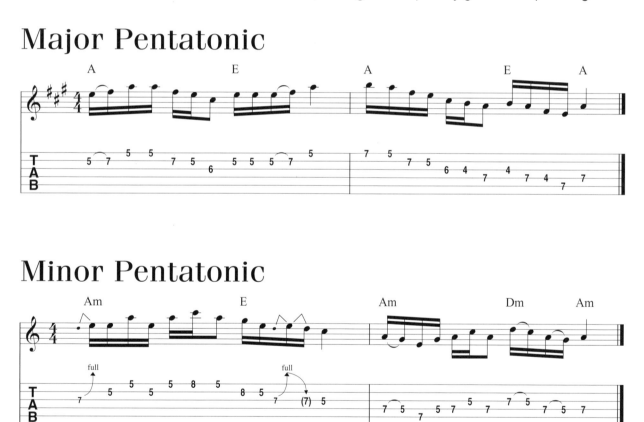

In general, try playing the major pentatonic scale over songs in major keys; the minor pentatonic over songs in minor keys. Use a song's key signature or its chord progression to help you determine its key.

Unusual Chords

Here are some less common open-position chords to wrap your fingers around. These are good fun to practice when you need a break from barre chords. Generally speaking, you can substitute these for the more common open position major chords.

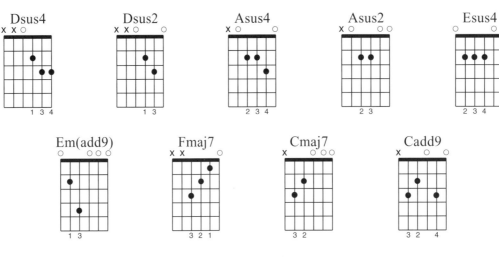

Inspiration

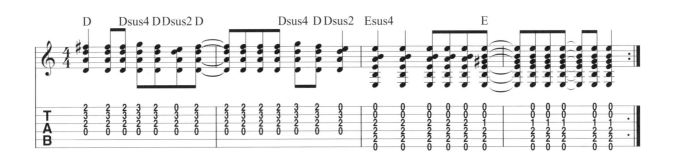

Open Strumming

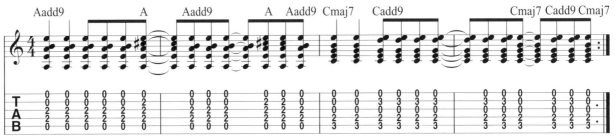

As you've no doubt noticed, these aren't too different from the major shapes we've already learned. Feel free to develop your own chords by taking an existing shape and changing a note here and there, and see what you come up with.

Three-Note Chord Forms

Track 195 Finally, here's one more antidote to "barre chord"-itis. These three-note shapes are all movable—just like barre chords—but they're much easier to play. Being on the top three strings, they also have a thin, cutting sound which makes them ideal for some rhythm guitar styles.

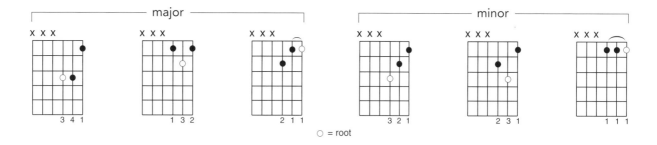

Pay attention to the root in each voicing; it tells you what chord you are playing. (The root will be on one of the top three strings—not necessarily on the bottom.)

Reggae

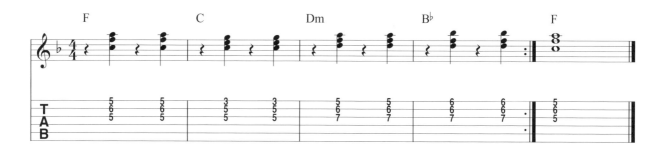

Fragments

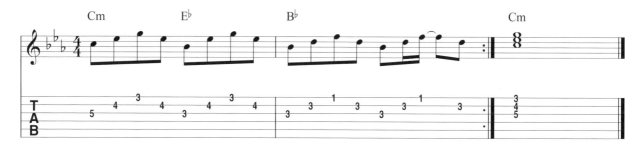

Review
Notes on the Fretboard

Notes in Fifth Position

Chords and Shapes

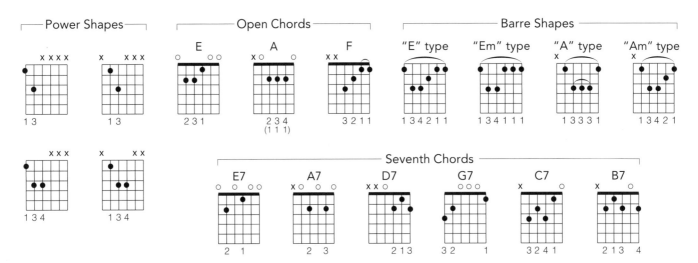

┌── Power Shapes ──┐ ┌──── Open Chords ────┐ ┌──────── Barre Shapes ────────┐

E   A   F   "E" type   "Em" type   "A" type   "Am" type

┌──────── Seventh Chords ────────┐

E7   A7   D7   G7   C7   B7